What folks are saying

Air Raid Nights and Radio Days by Don Schroeder is a return to innocence—an impressive coming–of–age novel, spanning the late '30s through the '50s…a finely–woven tapestry of life when family was strong, children sought out fun on their own, and goodness and morality reigned supreme.

—Susan R. Morrow, Ph.D., Professor Emerita, Southern Polytechnic State University, Marietta, GA

Milkmen, ice men, electric streetcars and front porches; the fact that few women drove cars, the corner grocery store with deliveries by bicycle [bring to mind] a different era.

—Judith La Fourest, Past National President, National League of American Pen Women

... Some great reminiscences.... In many of the stories one can see corollaries to present–day choirboy mischief!

—Frederick Burgomaster, Organist and Choirmaster, Christ Church Cathedral, Indianapolis

Air Raid Nights and Radio Day is an absolute treasure! People of all ages will enjoy this poignant, humorous, inspirational look at growing up in America's heartland before and after World War II. As a home school mother of daughters, ages nine and thirteen, and a director of our Christian home school cooperative, I urge you to add this wonderful book to your family's home school library.

—Karen K. Meister, Lake Elmo, MN

The stories of growing up in the very same neighborhoods I serve today are more than reminiscent—they still hold true. Kids still roam those streets and parents still struggle.... My organization... has a History & Preservation Committee.... So you can imagine the interest this book sparked for my group.

—Tracy Heaton de Martinez, Executive Director, Near East Side Community Organization, Indianapolis

I am pleased to salute this book as a delightful remembrance of the days when a young man munched on pieces of ice snatched from the back of a horse–drawn wagon ... climbed on backyard fences ... and even sang in a church choir.

—Keith L. Martin, Past President,
Indianapolis Literary Club

A pleasant journey back in time when life was simpler but not necessarily easier.

—Mary Watkins, Librarian, Yorktown High School, Yorktown, IN

To Rich —

Blessings abound!

Air Raid Nights
& Radio Days

Don Schroeder

Air Raid Nights & Radio Days

Hanging on for dear life

written by Don Schroeder
illustrated by Dan Mitchell

TATE PUBLISHING & Enterprises

Published by Tate Publishing & Enterprises, LLC
127 E. Trade Center Terrace | Mustang, Oklahoma 73064 USA
1.888.361.9473 | www.tatepublishing.com

Tate Publishing is committed to excellence in the publishing industry. The company reflects the philosophy established by the founders, based on Psalm 68:11,
"The Lord gave the word and great was the company of those who published it."

Book design copyright © 2009 by Tate Publishing, LLC. All rights reserved.
Cover and Interior design by Lindsay B. Behrens
Speaking bubbles by Lindsay B. Behrens
Illustrations by Dan Mitchell

Published in the United States of America

ISBN: 978-1-60696-034-9
1. Biography & Autobiography / Personal Memoirs
2. Humor / Form / Essays
09.01.29

Dedication

First, my hat's off to Dan Mitchell, this book's illustrator, who fleshed out and drew smiles on these exploits. Special thanks also to Dan's parents, Jim and Mary Liz Mitchell, who devoted many hours helping with the early manuscript!

Thanks to our children Glenn, Christy and Cindy for their encouragement. Thanks also to all who read the manuscript and offered helpful and critical insights, such as our neighbor Laura Hall, and, of course, Angela Faulkner, Tate Publishing's conceptual editor. Finally and especially, thanks to Helen for her support every blessed day. She was the computer brains behind the effort. Without Helen's assistance, this book would still be frozen on an ancient word–processing disk.

The characters in the book are real, but most of their names have been altered to avoid any embarrassment. Stories are based upon recollections of how life used to be. And sometimes the corners of those memories needed rounding out. Expect these stories to be nearer to reality than President Harry Truman believed when he said, "Things ain't like they used to be, and chances are they never were."

—D.L.S.

Table of
Contents

Foreword

Air Raid Nights and Radio Days by Don Schroeder is an exciting slice of life I could not put down. Whether the reader is from the older generation like the author, reliving World War II blackouts and polio breakouts, or my younger generation, learning about daily ice delivery, rag merchants and cootie–catchers, this anecdotal, fast–moving journey through Middle America is eye–opening. It will simultaneously bring laugh–out–loud and eye–watering moments. With poignant vulnerability, Schroeder's vignettes inform without preaching and inspire with humility and humor. You won't be disappointed.

—Dr. Paul W. Kummer
Pastor, Grace Lutheran Church, Destin, FL

Preface

This book looks at a slice of life in Middle America, from the close of the Great Depression through World War II, the postwar era and into the fifties.

America's birthrate significantly declined during the Depression. People like the author who were born during this era grew up to be categorized as part of the Passive or Silent Generation. Indeed, they fostered no student movement, nor did they complain about life as they found it. More accurately, they should be called the Thankful Generation. Their thankfulness was directed, of course, to the Greatest Generation—those who fought and in many cases died so their children could live in freedom. After the war, that same dedication that brought America victory went to work, creating a better life for us. How could anyone who inherited such a legacy complain or not be grateful?

It's said "We are what we were, when," meaning our character was mostly formed during our growing–up years. After the hardships of the Depression and World War II, conditions improved in virtually all ways as life opened up for this new generation of Americans. The times these people grew into were in sharp contrast with childhood memories.

Looking back upon the lifetime achievements of these millions of "silent" people, one realizes that on the darkest night the stars shine so brightly you can almost touch them. Encouraged by an improving life, this generation of Americans reached out with hope toward their dreams.

Young River

Young rivers rush from highlands, swift,
Boisterous, headlong, straight,
without a care they plunge,
Ineffable might,
In hopes we'll think they really know,
Their pathways out of sight.

Old rivers meander, lingering, slow,
Heading west then east, on table land they wind,
Inexorable night;
From destiny of ocean vast,
They seek to change their flight.
(Anonymous, Young River)

What has four wheels and flies?

Jammy said first things are important.

She said people steer boats across the ocean every day, but they don't make the newspapers because they aren't first. Columbus made all of the papers and history books because he was first to do it. She was right, of course. So I figured my first recollection must be worth something.

It had to do with Jammy's cat, which was gray and fat. My family was living in the first of two State Street houses. I must have been barely old enough to walk down the stairs, and probably not without holding on. The cat and I were upstairs. Downstairs dinner was nearly ready.

I recall picking up the cat and starting down the steps. Below, I saw my father reading the evening newspaper (The *Indianapolis News* was his paper). After about three steps, the cat grew tired of my plans with a leap. And I went tumbling.

My grandmother liked cats, candy, hot fudge sundaes, her only child (my mom), Aunt Mattie (my grandmother's life–long friend—the "Aunt" was honorary) Mrs. Roobush, and the memory of my grandfather. He had been a redheaded train engineer—the big boss on a passenger train during the early 1900s when trains were as important and romantic as anything had ever become in this country. That was before his taste for Irish whiskey sent him to an early grave. Of course, she also liked her grandchildren.

I called my grandmother "Jammy." Adults called her Jam, which is what I called her too by the time I was in high school. A grandchild had called her something that sounded like "Jammy" while learning to talk. And the name stuck. She was four feet six and as petite as her diet was picky. The older she got, the shorter she became, or so she claimed. She always made this claim when somebody mentioned her height.

When troubled by arthritis, scrapping grand-sons or bad news, she would say, "This world, then the next." That was one of many things about her upon which you could depend. When it snowed, you could bet she would tell about "back when it really snowed" in the 1880s.

"Mattie would come over and say, 'Let's go sledding.' Me and my brother, Volney, would get bundled up and take our sleds to the big hill on College Avenue. One of the boys would stand in the middle of Washington to watch for mule carts. (Washington Street was the National Road, U.S. 40). It was a great hill," she'd tell us as the memory of it filled her eyes.

"And with a good run, you could slide all the way across Washington Street."

Aunt Mattie was my grandmother's lifelong chum. Each had one child, both daughters. They were born within a few hours of one another and were known as "the twins." My Mom, Martha, and Aunt Mattie's daughter, Mary, also were life-long best friends.

In the 1830s, Jammy's mother's family had moved to Indiana from Virginia, where it was popular to name daughters after the state of their birth. My great grandmother was their first Hoosier child, and they named her Indiana. Jammy, whose baptismal name was Julia Goddard, was Indiana's youngest child.

While our first State Street house holds only a few memories, the second is full of them. Living in that second house, my life was too full to get my arms around. My world was a small one, though, bounded by State Street to the east, Sturm Avenue to the north, Vermont Street to the south and the alley behind State to the west.

My buddies and I mostly oriented to the alley.

Monday was garbage day, and that meant Benny and I could see a mule. Benny Jones and I would sit on the retaining wall over the alley and wait.

Benny had an artesian nose. Twin streams oozed onto the creases below each nostril, over his upper lip and into his mouth. Dirt defined the outer limits of each stream. A tad older than Benny, I figured I'd always known to use my sleeve. Benny didn't bother with such details.

By midmorning the garbage men's route brought them behind our house.

"Hi girls," they would always say to us. "We aren't girls. We're boys," we'd respond in unison with equal dependability and unoriginality. But this answer always caused the garbage men to howl with laughter. In 1941, five-year-olds could be counted upon to say nothing clever, unexposed as we were to television.

The garbage wagon was V-shaped, rusty, and pulled by a mule.

Rancid garbage invited clouds of buzzing, greenback flies. A slot opened at the bottom of the V to enable the garbage to slide out at the dump. People burned everything that would burn to make the garbage men's job easier.

Our garbage men were black and friendly and the only black people I had ever seen. "What has four wheels and flies?" was the first joke I recall understanding, thanks to the garbage wagon.

The iceman had a horse. Every house on State Street had ice cards, one foot square, placed in alley-facing windows to tell him how much ice to deliver for each icebox. The huge blocks of ice had grooves where they could be split into blocks of manageable weight. The iceman used a wedge and mallet to fracture ice into twenty–five–pound blocks. He used tongs to carry the ice over his shoulder. The ice sat on the wagon bed covered with a tarpaulin to help keep it from melting. The ice wagon was far more popular with neighborhood boys than the garbage wagon.

As soon as the iceman was out of sight with his delivery, we were onto the back of the wagon as fast as we could climb. We grabbed the biggest hunks we could hold and sucked and gnawed until we had nothing to show for it but clean hands and clean stripes where the water had run down our dirty arms.

It was part of our boy code that we never climbed on the ice wagon within eyeshot of the iceman. We not only waited until he was out of sight before climbing on, but we also were sure to be off the wagon before he returned.

While he may have wondered where we boys got our ice, he never let on like he thought we might have swiped it from him.

*It was part of our boy code that we never climbed
on the ice wagon within eyeshot of the iceman.*

Milkmen who delivered on State Street also
had horses but didn't use the alley. Benny's
mother ordered from Polk's Milk and we bought
from Banquet. Most days, the arrival of the milkman failed to arouse much interest.

The milkman picked up empty quart-glass
bottles and placed full ones in the milk box next
to our front door. On hot days, Mom or Jammy
would promptly transfer the milk to the icebox.

But on the coldest winter days, they took their good sweet time.

After several hours on such days, bottles of milk grew a five-inch cylinder of pure ice cream. They hadn't come up with homogenization, so the cream naturally floated to the top of the milk. When it froze, iced cream pushed the cap off the bottle. This was a treat too good not to share with the entire family, and with a harvest of three quarts of milk, there was some for everybody. We always sprinkled sugar on top.

Garbage collectors, milkmen, and icemen could have used trucks instead of mules and horses. However, many trucks were placed in storage because of a shortage of gasoline. Trucks were used when a route was too far from the barn for a horse or mule to travel in the allotted time. Gasoline was severely rationed during World War II so the United States military would have enough petroleum for their jeeps, ambulances, tanks, airplanes and ships.

"Rags...any rags today? Ragman! Ragman!" The ragman's raspy chant matched his red face, scrawny neck, and dirty, ragged clothing as he whipped the skinny horse that pulled his wagon.

Sometimes Birdy, our neighbor to the south, would have a bag or two of old dresses and trousers for which she would garner a few pennies. But mostly our alley was slim pickings for the ragman. In most of the houses on State, clothes were handed down or worn until they were threadbare. Then they were cut into cleaning rags.

The ragman bought old metal items until World War II, when everybody gave old metal to scrap drives. During the war, the ragman sold his collection of old clothes and rags to a paper company beside the White River near downtown Indianapolis. At that time, Indianapolis was the largest city in the United States not on a navigable river.

Rag pickers were even poorer than most of the women from whom they bought rags. And the one I remember was mean. Instead of waving at us boys who ran to see the horse, he would glare at us as though we were at fault for his misery.

The rag picker's horse was skin and bones. Once, while Benny and I were watching, his horse slipped going down an incline where our back alley ran into Sturm. The driver climbed down, screaming at the horse. Then he whipped it, commanding it to stand, but the horse could not because of downward pressure from the heavy wagon.

The ragman continued to whip the horse, screaming at it all the while. After a time, it was apparent even to a small boy the horse would never stand again. Stopping occasionally to catch his breath, the man continued to whip the dead animal.

After that, whenever the ragman glared at us boys, we glared right back.

People say: "I may forget a name, but I never forget a face."

The way faces grow up, age, get fat, grow beards, have hair turn gray or fall out, I don't understand how they do it. I forget both names and faces, but one thing I never forget is smells. And when I smell that same odor again, I can tell you when and where I smelled it before.

A path angled through a patch of weeds at the end of Birdy's backyard and ran into the alley. Late–summer weeds bloom with purple, yellow and white flowers and blend to give off a warm narcotic perfume. Forty years from that weed patch, I happened to have a cup of jasmine tea. The aroma of the tea transported me to that path through weeds grown higher than the eyes of a five–year–old.

It may be that all grade schools smelled alike in 1942, or maybe each had its own odor. But I'll not forget the smell of Indianapolis Public School 14 in the twelve–hundred block of East Ohio Street. It was a mixture of white paste, which was good to eat, disinfectant the janitor used on the floor, kids who didn't get Saturday night baths like most of us did, toilets and the gym.

My brother, Fred, and Benny's cousin, Dick Leary, had told Benny and me what awful places schools were supposed to be. Dick was wiry but strong and really smart. Being a couple of years older, he made it his business to look out for Benny and me. Dick and Benny went to Trinity Lutheran School on Arsenal Street, while my brother and I went to School 14. Each school was a little more than a half–mile's walk from where we lived.

Jimmy Hanks was the only one to cry my first day of school. I figured Jimmy had been filled in on the same stuff my brother had told me about, so I didn't blame him for crying. I was too scared to cry. But our teacher, Miss Kimberlin, was very nice to Jimmy and seemed pretty nice all the way around.

What my brother had told me, and what somebody must have told Jimmy, was that the principal, Mr. Thornburg, used a special paddle on unruly boys. The paddle had nails sticking out of it. Nobody I knew had actually seen the paddle. And though there were vague rumors, none of my friends ever got paddled with it. But fear of this device kept us more or less in line.

Older kids told of a boy who ended up crippled after being paddled with the device. But Fred told me not to believe everything I heard.

Kids in my class were not anywhere close to perfect, though none of us ever got paddled. The chewing of gum was forbidden. Despite dire warnings, many of us chewed gum when we could get it, quickly swallowing the wad when a teacher looked in our direction. We continued swallowing it even after the school nurse warned it would stay in our stomachs, forming a big ball which would have to be surgically removed. Maybe we worried less about swallowing chewing gum, because we seldom received more than a quarter of a stick. At the cost of a nickel a pack, parents made chewing gum go as far as possible.

When we could write, we also passed notes in classrooms (forbidden) and talked on the way to the gym or to the schoolyard (also against the rules). Though we were scolded, we escaped any real punishment.

A major benefit of being a pupil at School 14 was Miss Snodgrass, the visiting school nurse (who had warned of stomach chewing gum balls). Miss Snodgrass was plump, with a frowny, pink–skinned face. She wore white shoes, white see–through stockings, a white dress and half of a white hat pinned to the front of her hair. When she visited she came to our first grade classroom with helpful survival information.

First, we practiced a polite *"Good Morning, Miss Snodgrass."*

"That's so quiet I can't hear you," she responded. "Again!"

"Good Morning, Miss Snodgrass."

"That's much too loud. It's rude to be so loud. Again!"

"Good morning, Miss Snodgrass."

"That's much better."

Then we learned how to blow our noses.

It was to Miss Snodgrass a matter of life and death that nose blowing be done properly. We learned to shove in one nostril at a time while blowing into a tissue. I for one had been doing it wrong, blowing as hard as I could through both nostrils at the same time, until Miss Snodgrass came to my rescue.

We also learned dire consequences would result if we slept in our underwear, which many of us first confessed with raised hands that we did, instead of sleeping in pajamas which, judging from an absence of raised hands, no one in our class used.

Billy Bush said he didn't wear anything at all when he went to bed and wanted to know if that wasn't better than wearing underwear.

Miss Snodgrass deferred on answering Billy, opting to move to the next part of her lesson, despite a waving hand from Johnny Livingood, whom I figured had a really good answer for Billy. Johnny and I were buddies, and he was just as skinny as I was.

"Someday you will get sick at school," she warned. "As soon as you start to feel sick, politely raise your hand and tell the teacher that you need to throw up. Miss Kimberlin will excuse you," she told us, "whereupon you should walk quickly—do not run—to the boys' or girls' room where you should head to the closest toilet, raise the seat and throw up, taking care to channel the flow into the water, not onto the sides of the toilet.

"Now children, if you do not let Miss Kimberlin know right away that you need to throw up, you will run the risk of throwing up right next to your desk in front of everyone.

"And that would be embarrassing to you and will make a big smelly mess for the janitor to clean up," Miss Snodgrass advised.

"Now, then … are there any questions?"

Johnny Livingood's hand had continued waving throughout her dissertation on vomiting etiquette.

"I have to throw up," Johnny said when Miss Snodgrass finally responded to his raised hand.

Johnny Livingood's hand had continued waving throughout her dissertation on vomiting etiquette.

True to his word, he stood and proceeded to heave a vile orange and yellow stream all over pretty Suzy Caldwell, who had the misfortune to have been assigned the desk in front of Johnny.

The janitor arrived with sawdust, dustpan, broom, mop, disinfectant and a bucket of water. But he was of no help to Suzy.

After school, Benny, Dick and I prowled the neighborhood, looking to shoot dead anything or anybody who remotely resembled Hitler or his soldiers. Sometimes Fred joined us.

We wore civilian clothing so nobody would suspect us as being soldiers. During warm weather, we wore short pants, gray ankle–high sneakers and short–sleeve shirts. Our long rifles were cleverly disguised as sticks. Despite our non–threatening appearance, our assaults brought terror and awe to the faces of the enemy.

A man wearing a black shirt (an obvious Nazi) and patrolling with a German shepherd, jumped in fear from our loud frontal attack. We withdrew rapidly before he could call for back–up or even release his barking dog.

We used hunks of soft, orange brick or chalk to draw "KILROY WAS HERE" symbols on sidewalks, walls, and garages.

American soldiers drew the Kilroy symbol all over Europe. And just like GIs, we drew a straight line which represented a fence, and above the fence line we drew the top of a round bald head high enough above the fence that you could see Kilroy's two beady eyes. Kilroy had a big bulbous nose that hung down over the fence as did the fingers of his two hands. It was like you'd better be careful because Kilroy was watching! Under each drawing we printed: "KILROY WAS HERE." Kilroy struck fear in the hearts of Nazis everywhere.

Plumbing was nonexistent on our excursions, and it became our habit to urinate at the rear of the Roobush house. We were too short to be seen from inside the house; a wall and garage hid us from two other directions. So we only had to post a watch at the alley to ensure privacy.

We liked Mr. and Mrs. Roobush; it was just the best place to pee we could find.

Mrs. Roobush was my grandmother's best friend in Indianapolis. (Aunt Mattie now lived in Baltimore). Mr. Roobush had been a brick layer and had built their house himself. The brickwork was beautiful even to someone who knew as little as myself about the subject.

We continued using this field latrine for about a month while hunting the enemy. Though the acrid urine really stunk, Dick said our utilization of this facility was a way for the Roobushes to help with the war effort.

Neither the Roobushes nor Jammy saw it that way.

Without warning, Jammy asked me if my friends and I had been peeing on the Roobush house. I hung my head and said nothing, trying to think how to tell the truth without getting me and my friends in trouble.

Mom had always told me that "honesty is the best policy." Fully believing this, I had never lied about anything. But I had not been in such a spot before, either.

"Why don't you ask Freddie?" was what I finally came out with.

It turned out that she had already questioned my brother, and he had not handled the inter-rogation much better than I had.

While my grandmother was in no position to conscribe neighbor boys for a work party, she had no such problem with my brother and me. We found ourselves carrying and sloshing buckets of water onto the back of the Roobush house then sweeping the water away, until the stench dissipated.

Being sick was part of growing up. Dick was the only kid around who was sick more than me. He had recovered from rheumatic fever and his family was left worrying that he might have a damaged heart. (I overheard Jammy telling Mom about it one day, and it really worried me too, because Dick was such a good friend). Dick, Benny, Fred and I had all the other diseases that used to work their way through children until finally we were immune to just about everything.

Dick was to give me much over the years, but I didn't like his first gift, which was the mumps. After a short time, I passed the mumps along to my brother. We spent our convalescence whacking each other alongside the head with pillows.

Being hit in the jaw with a pillow hurts a good deal more if you have the mumps than if you don't. We couldn't have explained why, but we continued swinging away at each other.

We missed a lot of school because of the mumps. In the same period, I went through the chicken pox, scarlet fever, whooping cough and measles, plus tonsillitis every other month. Sore throats, colds and earaches attended me as well as toothaches. In the second grade, I was kept back a half grade so I would be sure to learn those aspects of the three Rs that I otherwise would have missed.

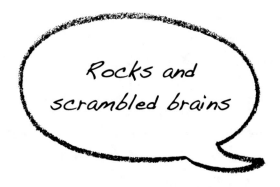

Rocks and
scrambled brains

Hitler was the worst person who ever lived, we
came to know. But Tojo was second, Benny and
I discovered.

"You know what the Japs do?" Dick Leary
asked us.

"They take little babies and stick pins into the
soft spots in their heads and it kills them!" he
reported.

"They found a whole mess of them. And they
couldn't figure out how Tojo had killed them
until they noticed those pinholes. Uncle Red told
me." You could tell by Dick's face, this horrified
him. He had a baby cousin he loved to hold and

talk to. I had never held a baby and would have been afraid to try.

We also learned lots of terrible things about Hitler and Tojo from newsreels at the Strand Theater, a neighborhood movie house on Washington Street, just west of Oriental Street. I was convinced that if we started losing the war and the Japs and Nazis came to Indianapolis, they would drag us all into the street, stick pins into babies' heads and shoot the rest of us.

We heard in detail how the enemy tortured American prisoners.

"They make them strip naked, and then they tie them down and poke electric cords into their ears and up their noses," Fred explained.

"Then they put red–hot irons on their bodies to torture information out of them."

But we knew that no American GI had ever given one shred of information to the enemy.

Their bravery amazed me. I knew I would not be brave if I were tortured. I felt unworthy to be an American.

Blue Star pennants hung in windows along State Street proudly telling passersby about a son or daughter serving in the military. The Mortons, a neighbor family one block south on State, had two stars, representing two sons fighting in the war. Only our neighbor Birdy displayed a Gold Star.

Birdy was a Gold Star Mother because her son, Buddy, was fatally wounded in the Navy.

She talked about Buddy at every opportunity as parents of deceased children do. I enjoyed hearing about him. So Birdy talked to me frequently about Buddy and what he had liked to do when he was a kid.

Buddy's favorite pastime had been fishing.

"His dad would take him out to the lake near where Jim grew up and they'd fish from a little boat. I think that's why Buddy wanted to be a sailor so bad," she remembered.

Birdy showed me pictures of Jim Jr. when he was about my age, in high school and then in his Navy uniform.

After we'd talked about Buddy one day, Birdy gave me all of his fishing gear. I was happy she gave it to me, but I felt unworthy of it. She predicted that with practice I would become as good at fishing as Buddy had been.

She said Buddy loved music and that he had lots of Victrola records, mostly big–band recordings by Benny Goodman, like "Stompin at the Savoy" and "Body and Soul," as well as by Tommy Dorsey, such as "Tiger Rag," and "Ida, Sweet as Apple Cider." Then she told me to wait where I was, which was sitting on a wooden box under Birdy's backyard tree. Birdy's trees had white-washed trunks. It kept bugs off, she claimed.

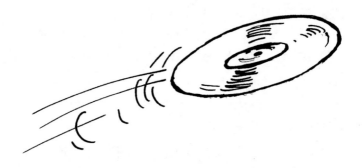

When she returned, she had a stack of Buddy's records.

"Let's have some fun," she said and instructed me how to hold a record on the edge and throw it like a Frisbee.

Birdy had come close to inventing the Frisbee long before Mr. Frisbee. We just didn't have the sense to realize it, but we sure had fun. Although the thick, black, soy plastic chipped all around the edges, the records didn't break. You could toss them, but you would hurt your hand if you tried to catch them.

We tossed them around the yard until Mom called for dinner.

My first real chance to help with the war effort presented itself at School 14. The school scrap drive was a huge event. We were urged to bring to school anything that contained metal, as much as we could carry, every day until the bins were full. Everybody used a can opener to remove both ends from tin cans of soup, fruit and vegetables, and then they smashed the cans flat. These were saved for scrap drives. Most families had several boxes full of flattened cans to donate.

We also brought all the toys from home we could sacrifice. I had a big red train engine I still sometimes rode. It contained more steel to help win the war than anything I owned except my tricycle. So I decided to donate the train engine.

Riding that engine eight blocks to school was out of the question, so I carried it, stopping every fifty feet or so to rest and to make certain I still had fingers.

All of that stopping and finger checking took a lot of time. My brother had long since left me behind. In fact, nobody else was in sight by the time I was a block or so from school. Then I realized I'd be late, which was a major School 14 transgression. A few hundred yards down the street I noticed a big eighth–grader standing in front of the school watching my slow advance.

"Here," I said to the boy when I finally reached him. It was his job that morning to accept steel bin contributions.

"Hey, okay!" he said, easily throwing the engine into one of the bins. "If every kid brought something as big as this, all these bins would be full." What he said really made me feel good!

"Now we'd better hurry. The tardy bell rang five minutes ago." The boy walked with me to my room and told the teacher why I was tardy— about the big train engine I had contributed and how heavy it was. Being tardy for such a good reason was okay, I learned.

Painted on an inside school wall was the outline of a Red Cross ambulance that looked like an unused coloring book picture. It was painted floor to ceiling, close to the principal's office, near where the steps ascend to the second floor. The black outline was gradually filled in, mostly with olive–drab paint from the wheels up, as the weeks went by and we bought enough War Bonds to pay for the vehicle.

Those who could afford it bought bond stamps for a quarter. We licked the stamps and stuck them on pages of our stamp book until every page was filled. A full stamp book equaled $18.75, which we exchanged for a $25 War Bond.

Uncle Sam advertised War Bonds through every possible media. There was one radio jingle I remember well:

"Any bonds today? Bonds of freedom that's what I'm selling. Any bonds today? Here comes the freedom man asking you to buy a share of freedom today!"

Including bonds that teachers bought, School 14 provided the Army with an ambulance and two jeeps before the war ended. We knew the ambulance would save the lives of lots of GIs. And the jeeps were really neat!

Everything seemed rationed in Mom's attempt to put food on the table. We only got a small ration of sugar. Butter was rationed but still too expensive for us. So Mom bought oleo.

Oleo started out white. Mom made it resemble butter by beating an orange powder into it. It was supposed to change into something that looked like butter. But ours was always sort of yellow, sort of white and streaked with orange.

The butcher displayed little meat. Not that we could have afforded much. Instead, we ate more than our share of liver, brains, tongue, heart and pig's feet. Among these delicacies, tongue was by far the best, with heart a distant second.

Mom stewed beef tongue with tomatoes, turnips, carrots and celery. It tasted wonderful. We didn't let the sight of white taste bud-covered skin get in our way of a great meal. We knew that the best meat you'd ever want to eat was right under that skin. So we just cut it away and dug in!

Brains were the pits, however. Mom scrambled eggs into the brains, which lent a yellow tinge to an otherwise gray glob. She said it helped make them taste better. I wasn't so sure. I tried closing my eyes so I didn't have to look at it. But even that didn't help.

I really liked "city chicken," which we sometimes got to eat. City chicken was chicken parts ground up with meal and formed on a wooden stick to resemble a drumstick. Mom fried it in lard.

Dick and Benny's grandmother made chicken and dumplings, which they told me about in detail. She obtained the chicken on rare occasions from a farm lady she knew. Up to that point I had never eaten real chicken, but it sure did sound tasty!

However, my idea and Dick's of something good to eat didn't agree on one thing.

Benny and I watched for burnt kitchen matches—the wooden kind, as we patrolled the alley behind State Street. We'd find them for Dick who loved to nibble the blackened sulfur ends.

"It's something his system needs, that's all," is how Jammy explained it.

Once, when Benny and our landlord's kids, George and Vance, and I found some burnt matches for Dick, he shared them with us.

"They're really good," he promised. We tasted the black end and spat it out. It was salty and gritty. I knew right away it wasn't anything my system needed.

If I had thought burnt matches would have made me play marbles as well as Dick or helped me to throw rocks with his accuracy, I'd likely have eaten them.

Throwing rocks was a vital skill for kids living on State Street. That's because we never knew when we'd be attacked by a rock-throwing gang of boys who lived on Arsenal Street, the next street to the west.

All we could do was take cover and return fire. Luckily, with each attack, Dick and my brother were with me, along with Benny and sometimes George and Vance.

I took a big rock in the center of my forehead once, just as I stood to throw. It became blue and knobby and looked like a budding horn.

Benny was wounded two or three times, once bad enough to upset his mother, not to mention Benny himself. We fought back from behind garbage cans and stockpiled rocks which we threw when we could get a shot. We held back the rest to ward off a frontal attack.

Once, Dick saved the day by filling his shirt front with rocks and, with a war cry, running and throwing well–aimed shots. You should have

seen those Arsenal guys run. Boy did they high–
tail it!

We cheered Dick and joined in the chase, hurl-
ing the rocks we'd saved, which usually landed
thirty feet behind the slowest boy.

"Blackhead" was our clever name for the largest,
oldest and meanest of the Arsenal Street bunch.
He had an unruly head of black hair and his face
was always dirty. My brother, who was in his
classroom, said his face was full of blackheads.

Blackhead also found his way into my nightmares, usually assaulting me with rocks. He
must have been eleven or so and was king of his
realm.

Dick had an idea we hoped would end the rock–throwing once and for all.

He cooked it up with Fred. Then they recruited the Stocktons, one Dick's age and the other my brother's age, five years my senior. Judging from their size, the Stocktons put away the potatoes.

It was arranged with Blackhead at school.

The State Street boys would play football against the Arsenal gang Saturday morning on a wide grassy strip which divided traffic on Sturm. We called it "the boulevard."

The way Fred explained it to Blackhead was this: "Throwing rocks is kids' stuff." We would play football to decide who was better. The loser would be able to challenge again next year, but in the meantime the winning group was neighborhood champ.

We got there first—me and Fred, Dick, Benny, as well as Larry Dean, one of their cousins, George and Vance, and the Stocktons. The Arsenals showed up with their usual contingent plus two older boys I had never seen.

The way we won the game had something to do with Dick throwing the ball to Fred or Larry. But it had a lot more to do with him handing it to the younger Stockton while the older one knocked down anyone in their path.

Most of us played line, and I spent much of the game under five hundred pounds of boy blubber. The Stocktons ran over or through anyone in their way, which even included Benny, George, and me.

And whenever Blackhead or one of his mates carried the ball, the Stocktons made them pay with heavy tackles and pile–ons. Our victory was major, something like sixty to six. The Arsenals' only score came when Blackhead pitched a lateral just before he was smashed by the biggest Stockton.

The trouble was we beat them too soundly. Because they weren't stupid, the Arsenals had no desire to play football with us again. But it wasn't long before small groups of us once more were attacked with rocks, "kids' stuff" or not.

President Roosevelt claimed we had "nothing to fear but fear itself." I had so many fears I had no idea what he was talking about.

To me, the 1930s and '40s were the dying years.

A sister and brother of mine died before I was born. Joan, the youngest of three sisters, and David, the second of three boys (all younger than the sisters) died when they were toddlers. After the second death, an autopsy was called for, which showed David died from a chronic lack of calcium.

In addition to Mom, Dad, Jam, Fred, and me, our family included my two older sisters, Mary Frances and Dorothy—or had included them. Both were married before the rest of the family moved to the second State Street house.

After David's death, Mom's number one goal had become to pour gallons of milk down Fred's throat and later mine as well. When I was about three, I was allowed to have some coffee and sugar in my milk so I would drink more of it. By the time I was five, I was drinking coffee like everybody else.

But I kept drinking lots of milk as well. Calcium tablets, the size of three stacked quarters, became part of the daily regimen. Fred and I chewed and gagged down this sweetened chalk just before bed.

I considered Fred to be home free and his calcium tablets just a precaution. But I figured that I needed at least three more years to get beyond the dying time.

If calcium and war worries weren't enough, summer radio messages warned that one in ten would catch polio. Our President was crippled by it. And I knew it killed people too. To help raise money to treat polio, newspapers showed pictures of children trying to walk with crutches and children in iron lungs. I figured polio meant death, crutches or iron-lung imprisonment.

Tommy Barnett was a kid in my class at school who always seemed to be sick. He would attend school for a few days and then would be off for several weeks. He looked sickly when he attended school and always had a sad look about him.

One morning our teacher told us Tommy had died. I was not surprised. I think I had sensed he would die. I was sorry, but I didn't cry because I didn't really know him. Maybe I had stayed away from him, trying not to know him.

Another boy in my class, Johnny Rogers, had the prettiest mother in the world. It was not just looking at her that made her pretty, it was her looking at you! Her eyes joined up with her smile and said to me, "I really like you." I really liked her in return. Johnny's younger sister was very pretty, too. I thought someday she would grow up to be almost as pretty as her mother.

One day, Johnny came to school weeping. His mother had died the night before, and his dad had sent the children to school not knowing what else to do. Her dying made no sense to me, and being a child I wasn't told what caused her death.

I realized it was sad for a child like Tommy to die. But the saddest thing of all was for one of our mothers to die.

I also worried that Hitler or Tojo would bomb our homes.

The Civil Defense organization conducted nighttime blackouts or air-raid drills, so we would know how to prevent Indianapolis from being bombed to kingdom come.

Air–raid drills were publicized, and when it was dark wardens patrolled our neighborhood looking for lights. My folks always turned out all of our lights and refused even to burn a candle.

To pass the period between nightfall and going to bed, we turned on the radio and listened while sitting in the dark. During one air raid drill, *Fibber McGee and Molly* was playing and Fibber was about to open his closet, when a shout from a Civil Defense warden came up to our second-floor living room.

We were ordered by the angry–sounding warden to turn off the radio because bombers could spot the tiny light in the dial, and Indianapolis would be blown up. Jammy turned off the radio to the crash of Fibber opening his closet.

Not getting to hear the rest of *Fibber McGee and Molly* was little enough sacrifice. But I couldn't help but wonder why the enemy wouldn't be smart enough to bomb us during the day when they could see.

Jammy's oldest sister came to live with us after her husband died.

We all called her Aunt Lolly though she was Mom's aunt. It was her custom to gather me onto her lap and read aloud the obituaries in The *Indianapolis News.*

"You're going to scare that boy to death, always reading to him about dead people," said my father, who seemed not to like her.

Aunt Lolly had been married to Uncle Dolly, a heavy, red–faced man with a bushy mustache.

It seemed to me that Uncle Dolly and Aunt Lolly had traveled all of the time before he died.

They had no children but took full advantage of the hospitality of friends and relatives throughout the country, visiting for weeks at a time before moving on to another home.

While visiting, Uncle Dolly went door to door selling thread, which was how he made a living.

Uncle Dolly always kissed me upon his arrival and departure, so I could empathize with walruses. But now he was dead, and Aunt Lolly was taking final advantage of her baby sister's hospitality.

That wasn't careful thinking on her part. It was my parents not my grandmother who paid the rent and bought the groceries. And there was little enough money without one more mouth to feed. But people in those days said proudly, "We take care of our own."

Her arrival may have been the last straw for my alcoholic father.

He had lived through the Depression and the shame of long periods of joblessness, had buried two children and must have heaped guilt upon himself thinking the children hadn't had enough milk.

It's likely that in fact they did receive sufficient amounts of milk and calcium but suffered from a condition in which their bodies were unable to properly store the calcium. But Mom and Dad never knew that. Joan was an especially pretty child, and a dairy used a photograph of little Joan drinking milk in a newspaper ad. The ad was discontinued after she died.

When my father got to the point of drinking up money needed for family survival, Mom had no choice but to divorce him. It was likely the hardest thing she ever had to do. At my age, I knew nothing of parental separation or divorce. As nearly as I recall, my father would be gone all day—working I supposed—and also was gone most evenings. Then at one point he failed to reappear. I don't remember an explanation. He simply disappeared from our home and from my life.

My two sisters had jobs. But because they had gotten married while we were living in the first State Street house, they were no longer around to help with household expenses. However, once they had moved from our home, the cost of food was reduced and the family was able to get by with a smaller place—our second State

Street house. Mary Frances, my older sister, married an Italian immigrant, and Dorothy married her high school sweetheart who lived down the street. Each young man was exempted from military service because of physical problems.

After the divorce, Mom took in washing and did housework. And she set aside one day a week to look for better-paying work. But everywhere she went she was told, "We are looking for a younger girl," or simply, "Sorry, you're too old."

Mom was over 40. A woman at an employment agency gave her this advice: "You look ten years younger than you are. Just knock ten years off your age when you fill out employment forms."

The advice worked right away. Mom was hired for a job as an order clerk at the Kroger Grocery warehouse. She was to work there in the same job for well over twenty years taking orders from Kroger meat managers throughout Indiana.

When Mom was nearly sixty–five, she told her supervisor that in a few weeks she would be old enough to retire. She explained how the employment agency lady had advised her to take ten years off her age, and that now she was applying for retirement.

"You'll retire in a pig's eye," the man told her.

"Clean out your desk—you're fired."

Though Mom got not so much as a penny in pension, she continued to buy all of her groceries at Kroger Grocery stores. "He (the boss) was just one bad man. The rest of Krogers is good," was her explanation.

Mom didn't remarry for a number of years following the divorce. She considered herself lucky to have the job at Krogers, although the pay wasn't good. I remember her saying she made only $1,000 for an entire year, after working at Krogers for three or four years. But she was able to walk the mile to the Kroger warehouse from our house on State Street. And what she earned kept our family together.

Besides Mom, the family now included me and Fred, Jammy and Aunt Lolly. Jammy's cat had disappeared.

Aunt Lolly was well into her eighties and forgetful. She conducted what my brother considered a reign of terror on him.

He spent many hours building P-38s and other World War II fighter plane models out of balsa wood strips and tissue paper. For reasons I never understood, he often left the models under construction—wings, fuselages or even entire planes sitting on a chair for the banana–oil glue and damp tissue paper to dry.

Apparently, Aunt Lolly's vision was nearly gone, because she often sat on Fred's models. She must have smashed a half-dozen over a couple of years. He was certain she disliked him and was smashing the planes on purpose.

When Aunt Lolly was young, she and a sister-in-law went hiking with Aunt Lolly's seven–year–old nephew.

They were hiking along a railroad track, because that was a clear place to hike in the country. Somehow, the boy had gotten a foot wedged in a switch in the railroad track. They tried everything they could to free him but were unsuccessful. So the boy's mother and Aunt Lolly lifted their long dresses and ran in opposite directions up and down the track to wave down any approaching train.

A train soon came from the direction Aunt Lolly was running; she waved franticly at the engineer, but he was unable to stop in time, and the boy was torn apart.

Aunt Lolly continued having nightmares about it.

As progressive strokes and senility claimed much of her humanity, she lay in bed mumbling, "ohpoboyohpoboyohpoboyohpoboyohpoboyoh poboy..."

We understood her only because sometimes when she would become agitated, reaching out with urgent eyes she would clearly say, "Poor boy, oh poor boy, poor boy."

I had a dentist, Dr. Horace Abdon, who was about to become a hero.

Drinking milk every time I turned around left a lot of glucose in my mouth and it caused cavities. So did the sweet calcium tablets I chewed up before going to bed. And with everything Mom was struggling with, my dental hygiene left something to be desired. Consequently, my first teeth were full of painful cavities. So by the time my second teeth came in, my toothbrush and I had become good friends.

While I was having so many toothaches, Dr. Abdon picked me up in his Model–A Ford, treated my toothaches, bought me an ice cream cone and took me home again. Getting to ride in a car was a big deal and he made my toothaches go away. But that wasn't why he was a hero.

Dr. Abdon stopped picking me up in his Model–A to join the Army.

He was sent to an island in the Pacific where the Japanese were well entrenched. He was assigned to an artillery unit to treat GIs' teeth. Artillerymen support the infantry and seldom lay eyes on the enemy unless the battle goes badly.

When the infantry in front of Dr. Abdon's forward observer unit started retreating all around, he knew he had problems. The artillery also should have been retreating. But the lieutenant in charge of the unit refused to issue a retreat order, despite the fact that Japanese foot soldiers had been spotted advancing.

When Dr. Abdon asked the lieutenant why they weren't moving out, he was told they would stay put until ordered to move. He even refused

Dr. Abdon's suggestion to apprise the commanding officer of the need to retreat.

This sounded like mass suicide to my dentist!

Dr. Abdon was a captain and outranked the lieutenant. However, doctors and dentists in the military have no field command authority.

Realizing that his life and the lives of many others hung in the balance, Dr. Abdon seized command from the lieutenant (with the cooperation of the men) and ordered the unit to collect all records and equipment and retreat.

Luckily, the Japanese failed to press their advantage.

As Dr. Abdon's forward observer unit moved to the rear, they came upon the main body of the artillery. He told the colonel in charge that the attacking Japanese were right on their heels. The colonel ordered artillery gun barrels lowered parallel to the ground and then ordered the artillerymen to fire on the Japanese.

Not only did Dr. Abdon save the lives of everyone in his unit, the order to fire on the advancing enemy badly crippled the Japanese offensive.

When Dr. Abdon reached the rear area, he went straight to the commanding general and told him he'd just committed a court-martial offense and explained what had happened.

The general was so impressed, he issued an order that Dr. Abdon receive the Silver Star for his heroism and all members of his unit (except the lieutenant) the Bronze Star. But my dentist said he hadn't done any more than anyone else and would accept only a Bronze Star.

While Dr. Abdon was away helping to win the war, our family followed his advice for inexpensive tooth care. We sprinkled baking soda and a little salt in the palm of one hand and dipped a damp toothbrush into it. The soda and salt stuck to the toothbrush real good. Soda and salt were the main ingredients of commercial toothpaste and tooth powder and cost next to nothing, he told us.

If you didn't like the salty taste and could afford it, nothing beat Dr. Lyon's Tooth Powder! Dr. Abdon claimed this tooth powder, in the familiar blue and white tin, cleaned and polished teeth without harming the enamel and was superior to commercial toothpaste sold at that time.

After the war, Dr. Abdon returned to his practice in the old neighborhood. He remained my dentist until he retired. He wouldn't take any money from Mom for working on my teeth. And as long as I went to him, he even refused to accept payment from me.

Instead, he'd say things like "You were my first patient, so you don't have to pay," or "You've been a patient of mine longer than anybody else, so there's no charge."

Nasty little gutter tramp

George and Vance lived downstairs from us and we paid rent to their parents. George was about my age and Vance a year or two older.

More than proximity, it was marbles that brought us together.

Marbles occupied my mind and much of my time for two long summers. It remains a mystery how a seven-year-old thumb and index finger could shoot a marble with any accuracy.

Extreme motivation had to have been behind it—motivation that comes from playing "keepers."

The league we played in centered in a circle of string on a side yard of hard–packed dirt between our house and Birdy's. We always played "keepers." That meant you went home with the other kids' marbles or they went home with yours.

The rules were simple:

First and foremost, no aggies (agate–weighted shooters) were allowed. You had to depend upon accuracy to knock marbles out of the ring. Any kid who tried to use an aggie would have been viewed as the worst kind of cheater. That's because an aggie will plow like a tank through a ring of marbles.

Each boy anted up by putting five marbles in the ring. And you were really dumb if you used shiny marbles instead of ones that were scratched and nicked (unless, like

George and Vance, all of your marbles were brand new).

Players started with a toss from a line ten feet beyond the circle; the closest marble to the circle shot first followed by others in the order of proximity; and if your shooter stopped in the circle, it cost you a marble and a trip back to the toss line. You always shot from where your shooter landed after your previous shot.

Fudging was outlawed. That meant you had to hold your marble exactly at the place it had come to rest after the previous shot. A player could not use elbow or wrist action when shooting to give a marble extra speed. However, all of us fudged as much as we could get away with.

Most importantly, any marbles you knocked out of the ring became your own personal property. And whenever you knocked out a marble, you got another shot.

Competitors besides me included Dick and Benny, George and Vance, and sometimes Fred or Benny's cousin, Larry.

Dick and Benny always brought sacks of scratched and nicked marbles for the circle, as did I. But the sons of my landlord invariably showed up gripping bags of clean, shiny, just-bought-at-Haag's drugstore marbles.

After several hours of competition, George and Vance's marbles were transferred to the possession of Dick, Benny, myself and most other competitors.

We played when it didn't rain. On rainy days, I counted and shined my marbles.

Next to getting an ice cream cone, my greatest joy came from initiating the transfer of Vance's marbles from his bright red bag to the old box I kept behind the davenport. Winning other people's marbles was fun but less so than taking Vance's.

It's doubtful that Vance had faults beyond those of most kids his age. As near as I can recall, with one or two exceptions, his biggest fault was that I didn't much like him.

First, you could be sure he would pick on George at every opportunity, even though his little brother was a pretty nice kid. And then he would grin, all satisfied with himself.

He must not have owned a toothbrush. Why else would his grins have been greenish gray?

Vance had a lifetime of crud growing on his teeth from his gums down almost to the jagged edge–line where the teeth ended. But it wasn't just his breath that gave him an aroma that kept you from wanting to be around him longer than necessary to win his marbles.

George said it was because Vance wet his bed every night, and each morning his mother scrubbed him with vinegar. So besides the rotten breath, Vance smelled like sour urine.

One evening when I was counting my marbles, Mom sat down next to me.

"Mrs. Snively" (that was our landlady) "told me that she is getting tired of buying marbles for George and Vance. She says that you boys take their marbles away from them."

"We don't take them away from them, Mom. We win them fair and square," I told her.

"Well, Mrs. Snively is very upset. Maybe you should stop playing marbles with George and Vance, or if you play, stop keeping their marbles."

"But Mom! That would take all of the fun out of it!"

"Well, I wish you would do what I said. It can be a favor, just for me."

I was certain Mrs. Snively was upset with me for winning away George and Vance's marbles. She was always mad about something. I don't recall what she looked like, but I sure can tell you how she sounded. She was always yelling! We lived above the Snively's and we frequently heard her screaming at George and Vance. She sometimes even yelled at Mr. Snively when he got home from work!

My mother seldom asked me for favors. So when she did, I wanted to do as she requested. But what she was asking seemed to violate a sacred boy code of conduct.

Besides, if I couldn't play keepers, what would I do for fun? I didn't know, but I went to sleep fully intending to quit marbles and take up some other game.

The next morning, Dick and Benny banged on our door.

"You should see George and Vance's big new bags of marbles," Benny reported.

"Get out here and let's play some marbles."

I was out as fast as I could grab my bag of banged up marbles, the ones I used for the circle.

George and Vance were there alright. They had even swept and marked off the course.

Benny hadn't exaggerated. Instead of the twenty–five–cent-size bags of marbles they had always shown up with, the Snively boys clutched brand new fifty-cent bags.

When a boy is seven and his mother asks him to do her a special favor and then he does just the opposite, he feels pretty rotten.

Guilt took up residence in my brain and stayed. But instead of hurting the way I shot, it seemed to improve upon it.

"Boy, you can't miss," was how Dick put it. If I said that Dick was the best marble player in Indianapolis, nobody I knew would have disagreed. But that day I played pretty well myself.

Oddly, Vance was knocking out more marbles than he ever had and was well into the game long after George's marbles were gone. I figured he was being lucky, though I wondered how he could be that lucky!

"Hold it," Dick shouted as Vance had knocked out two marbles with one shot. Then he grabbed Vance's shooter and studied it.

"He's using an aggie!" Dick shouted.

He passed the shooter around. Sure enough, inside the cloudy green glass was an irregular shape, an agate of lead. It was the heaviest shooter I had ever held.

"Okay, buster, we'll keep on playing, but you have to use a fair shooter," Dick ruled.

The game reverted to the marbles I knew and loved. Vance joined George at losing and the rest of us profited from his misfortune. An hour later, it was my honor to knock out the final marble which rolled to a stop in front of Vance.

"You dirty cheater" he yelled as he threw the marble at me.

Luckily, he was as bad at throwing marbles as he was at shooting them. Then the boy with the green teeth went crying into the house to tell his mother.

Winning at keepers with George and Vance was only one of my offenses. Another had to do with climbing Mrs. Snively's backyard fence.

The fence separated me from Dick and Benny, who lived in opposite sides of the next–door double.

When I was in the backyard, it was possible to walk along the side of the house and out to the front sidewalk in order to go next door and visit Dick and Benny. But the shortest route was across the backyard fence, and that's the route I always took.

Mrs. Snively seemed always to wait until I was at the very top of the fence before screaming:

"You dirty little gutter tramp, get off my fence."

I always obliged her, though in the process I somehow ended up on Dick and Benny's side. When you are on top of a fence, it doesn't hurt the fence any more if you jump to the destination side, instead of back to the side you were coming from.

And while I invariably did this and always tried to look as innocent as a newborn pup, I always felt guilty.

The day after scoring my big marble win, I was heading over the backyard fence to visit Dick and Benny when Vance's mother spotted me and screamed louder at me than she ever had:

"You nasty little gutter tramp, get down from my fence this instant!"

It must have been the shrill in her voice that froze me at the top of the fence. As she glared at me, I just stared back, all gape-mouthed.

Then I heard Dick's mother. She was standing at an upstairs bathroom window, open against the summer heat, her hair wet like she'd just washed it.

"You miserable old witch," she shouted. "Leave that boy alone!"

I had never heard Dick's mother raise her voice against anyone. Dick's mother was not the sort of person from whom I ever expected anger. She was beautiful and, now I realize, only in her middle twenties.

She was gentle too, especially with Dick who was a strong kid but was often sick with something. She also was very nice to Benny and was nice to me even though I wasn't a relative.

"Is that what she said?" I heard Dick and Benny's grandmother ask Benny's mom. Both were standing in their backyard taking all of this in, I saw from my perch astride the fence.

I climbed down into Dick and Benny's yard and ran—but not before seeing Mrs. Snively's face again. I had never been around unkindness or hate. But when I saw it in her eyes, I knew exactly what I was looking at. I figured I deserved it because of the fence and because I had not done what Mom had asked of me.

That evening, our family received an eviction notice. We were given a month to find another place to rent and to arrange for the move.

And so Mom began the difficult search for an affordable place to rent. The dwelling needed to be nearby so that Mom could walk to work and Fred and I wouldn't have to change schools.

Mom told me Mrs. Snively needed a place for her mother to live. But I believed that because I hadn't given up playing keepers with George and Vance and because I continued to climb the Snively fence, I was to blame for our family being evicted.

*You nasty little gutter-tramp, get down
from my fence this instant.*

He was down the sidewalk nearly a block away,
close to where a road–kill cat had stunk up the
place the summer before. There sat Vance on his

new red tricycle. I was on my hand-me-down tricycle. From my position he was a straight shot. Vance had his back to me, and he seemed to dawdle, slowly rocking back and forth a few inches in each direction. It looked like he was studying cracks in the sidewalk. "Step on a crack and you'll break your mother's back."

I didn't recognize what seized me because I had little understanding of theological concepts except that somehow "Jesus loves me, this I know for the Bible tells me so." I was years from learning about original sin, though I was about to demonstrate it.

My legs started to push harder and harder on the pedals, hurtling me forward faster and faster to a speed I had never before attained toward the target. Boy and machine moving through space as one until … impact.

The Morton's hedge begged to be trimmed, standing five feet tall in the August sun. I can still see Vance sailing over that hedge, landing in a tumble on the Morton's lawn.

It's frightening to recall how happy I was as Vance ran, screaming toward home. It hardly mattered that my tricycle (my favorite possession next to the box of marbles) ended up with a bent front wheel.

For a time after that it rode with a proud wobble, like a wounded soldier's limp. Then the wheel fell off.

I never played marbles again.

Pack up
your troubles

Finding an acceptable place to rent at a price Mom could afford was no easy matter. After looking for several weeks, Mom found a house within walking distance of her job and in the School 14 area so Fred and I wouldn't have to change schools.

The place she found had the necessary attributes. But it looked like a mistake to me.

Except for Aunt Lolly, we went together to see it. Our new residence on East Ohio Street was just a half block down from School 14. And Mom's walk to work was about the same distance as it had been from State Street. The rent was about the same as we had been paying, as well.

Like our State Street home, this one was an upstairs duplex, also with a separate front door. Our State Street residence had been small, and this one was considerably larger.

The main reason it looked like a mistake to me was cockroaches.

When we first saw it, I was certain this one house supplied Indianapolis with all of its cockroach needs. No one has ever believed my cockroach story. I expect nobody ever will. I would not believe such a story from someone else. But it's all true.

Every square inch of the floor of every room in the house contained at least one cockroach. And it was in the afternoon!

The confused roaches swarmed away from me this way and that, like schools of small fish, but I stamped hundreds to death. I would kill five or ten with each step, and I made it my business to jump about killing as many as possible.

Mom had a better idea. She bought a dozen canisters of blue poison and sprinkled it around the edges of every room.

Ten days later, when we returned to clean up prior to the move, not a single cockroach was in evidence. Even the ones I had killed had been cannibalized before the massive population disappeared behind walls and under floorboards to die.

Mom continued to place cockroach poison in out-of-the–way places as long as we lived in this house. Nevertheless, whenever we turned on a light in the middle of night, we'd spot one or two large brown roaches dashing toward the baseboard.

Our new residence was a massive gray structure, erected around 1890. It was just a mile from the center of the city. When built, it must have housed a wealthy family.

Now, the widow who owned the house refused to pay for improvements or even to help with the cost of the wall paint that Mom bought to brighten up the inside.

The house gave me the willies.

Cooing pigeons made ghostly noises from roosting places under sheltering eaves. A hundred generations of them had perched there and droppings had collected more than a foot deep.

On windy days we breathed the dust from it, and after rains we smelled its musty stench.

I frequently had the flu, tonsillitis, colds and other infections which hung on for weeks. But Dr. Hasslinger never mentioned histoplasmosis, a troublesome lung infection from breathing the dust of bird droppings.

The innards of the house shuddered and groaned. I came to learn these sounds were emitted from the basement when our downstairs neighbors shook ashes from their furnace and shoveled coal into its iron belly.

Even when I could identify the noises of our house, it whispered of evil somewhere under the surface. Childish imagination, one would suppose.

In a few years it became my job as it had been Fred's to tend our furnace. Four times a day I shoveled coal into the insatiable mouth of this red monster.

The first thing every morning, I shoveled out cooled ashes from the ash pit into galvanized containers for the trash man. Then I shook the hot ash down into the cooling pit and added more coal to the furnace. A person couldn't help coughing and gagging when working with ashes.

Every neighborhood house was heated with coal, mostly the high sulfur kind strip–mined in Indiana like we used. Winter air was yellow-gray from soot and sulfuric gas.

You could taste it when you breathed and again when you cleaned the black from your nose. Most everything became gray from coal soot and dust.

The earth was black from years of coal soot. Black soot with its oily content turned white houses gray. Sheets, white shirts and underwear hung out to dry on clotheslines soon were gray. It got on hands, smudging everything touched. Children's faces and hands were grayed from the oily black which permeated skin pores, defying soap.

Rings of scum remained in bathtubs on Saturday nights, and children climbed out only shades cleaner than before climbing in.

Even newly fallen snow turned gray within a few hours.

At school I heard about a terrible fire which had killed three of School 14's children.

I asked Fred to take me to see where the house on Oriental Street had burned. He told me to wait until the weekend. On Saturday it was snowing heavily. Fred and I put on boots and walked the few blocks to see what remained of the house. On the front lawn were mattresses, overstuffed chairs and a sofa. Fred guessed firemen had moved them outside because they were smoking so badly.

The furniture on the lawn lay every which way, but snow covered it all, giving chairs and sofa white shoulders. Heavily falling snow dimmed our vision of the roof. But I could see that part of it had disappeared.

In a few days, my brother and I returned to see the house. All the snow had melted to disclose the horror of things half burned.

A moist, charred smell filled my nostrils. That smell and the thought of burning death pumped bile into my throat. I couldn't rid my soul of it. Anything that smelled similar in the least, even chocolate, nearly made me ill. The West Bakery baked bread a few blocks from where we lived.

For months, the baking aroma of salt-rising bread, which was a popular bread at the time, also turned my stomach.

The attic in our house had nearly as much floor space as our residence. But it served only to collect dust and dirt. A brick-sided cistern, no longer in use, stood near one wall of the attic. I could squeeze between the cistern and a wall. That's where I would hide when the Nazis came.

I thought of the pigeons roosting outside attic windows as flying rats and came to hate them. They symbolized stench, filth and poverty. Flocks of them fed on garbage in the alley and on unseen specks of food in grass–barren yards, and so I threw rocks at them.

In time, I crippled two or three and felt badly on each occasion, knowing the birds were in misery. I would not have felt badly had I killed them outright.

The ceiling of the stairway leading to our home was an embarrassment. In places, the many layered wallpaper tore from the ceiling in the shape of devil wings. The stairway ceiling only could be reached with a scaffold, so we were unable to tear off the old paper.

These wallpaper shrouds also became a symbol for me of our poverty.

Many years later, this same house was inhabited by a criminal motorcycle gang. Gang members filled in the porch with concrete block, leaving holes from which to fire guns at rival gang members or the police.

When Indianapolis police armed with a search warrant were denied entry, a gun battle ensued. Tear gas finally cleaned out this rats' nest. Newspaper reports said all of the rooms were painted black to discourage police or others from seeing what was happening inside.

A neighborhood organization bought the derelict house from the city, restored and sold it. Under the umbrella of the Near East Side Community Organization, NESCO, this area is now known as the Holy Cross–Westminster Neighborhood. Holy Cross Catholic Church, with its elementary school, has been a strong pillar for the area over the years. Down the street from Holy Cross, my old house stands as a symbol of neighborhood revitalization. It is for me more than that. It is good rising up over evil.

Someone said about the years of the Depression and of World War II, "We were poor, but we didn't know it." Well, in my family, we knew we were poor. Poverty was nothing to be ashamed of, especially considering my family's circumstance. I felt shame, nonetheless.

In later years, I was ashamed to invite friends to my home, especially rich kids from church. And when the father of one of my friends kindly drove me home from some church function, I asked to be let out a good distance from my home so no one would see where I lived, or think of some excuse to come inside for a visit.

"Which house do you live in?" the father of a friend asked me one night in the dead of winter. "Oh, it's around the corner. But I'll just get out here. I feel like walking a little bit tonight," I responded. With the temperature hovering slightly above zero and the night wind howling?

I didn't tell anyone about my shame, least of all my mother who worked so hard for what we had.

Moving had been difficult for me, as it is for most any child. A child's family is half of his life. Neighborhood chums are most of the rest of it. My friends were too far away to visit on my own until I was ten or so and could afford a bicycle.

Despite our family's difficulties, I had my share of fun. Poor people and rich people are close to the same in happiness and sadness. It's just that rich people can be happy or sad in style.

For instance, I could have candy anytime I wanted it. A walk to the corner grocery store at the corner of Oriental and Ohio streets, just down the street, was worth a few pennies if I took the alley route, where I was almost certain to find a few empty soda bottles. With the money I got from turning in these bottles, I could buy four or five different pieces of candy.

Most people walked to the corner store with a grocery list that a clerk would use to collect everything they wanted. Our neighbors made several trips each week, so they seldom had more than a single bag to carry home. Food was fresher when promptly used after purchase, and a single bag of groceries was not too heavy to carry home. The store also took orders over the phone, and a boy delivered the groceries using a specially built bicycle that had an oversized basket above a small front wheel.

But in a couple of years, this corner grocery and others went out of business because of supermarket competition. In our neighborhood, a new green-fronted Kroger store opened on Washington Street just east of Oriental Street. (The Kroger Grocery chain later changed its corporate color from green to blue).

At first, Kroger customers also compiled lists for a grocer to fill. A few years later, the store converted to a small supermarket by rearranging the shelves and providing carts for customers' use in collecting their own groceries. Because the store reduced its labor costs, it reduced what it charged for groceries.

But our neighborhood drugstore stayed the way it was. We would tell a clerk the one or two things we wanted to buy, and he would get those items for us and ring them up.

To me, that was the way drugstores ought to be. When drugstores became vast markets where the customer is left alone to search high and low for one or two needed items, it seemed to me to be out of sync with the laws of nature and common sense.

Corner groceries disappeared without fanfare, almost without notice. In the same way, other pieces of neighborhood scenery were removed from the stage of my existence, as a setting for a play is updated to show the passage of time. For me, it was not really like that, because when you see a play, you understand the stage manager's handiwork. But I scarcely noticed, let alone analyzed, the changes around me.

A generation passes away one life and then another, until every wonderful, loving human being of the time is gone. Shallowly, newspapers print obituaries, but they fail to notice the great banner story, let alone to write it.

Red fire boxes were mounted on utility poles throughout every neighborhood. They were so numerous that if a house caught fire, a person could run a few hundred feet to the nearest fire box to summon fire engines. A small hammer hung from a chain at each box to break a glass plate on the face of the fire box. When the glass broke an alarm sounded at the nearest fire station.

The meanest kids in every neighborhood broke fire-box glass just to see the fire engines. There were many such false alarms in my neighborhood endangering everyone. When firemen were responding to a false alarm, they could not answer a genuine call for help. And, of course, the fire box needed to be rearmed.

At some point, fire boxes were removed. Was it because telephones came to be installed in nearly all homes or that fire boxes were used so often for false alarms?

Icemen also disappeared as people purchased refrigerators. I don't remember noticing.

Even milkmen stopped delivering milk to front doors of our neighborhood as mothers bought milk for less money at Krogers. Leaky wax-board cartons of homogenized milk replaced the kind milkmen delivered which did not leak—those quart size milk bottles, with an hourglass globe for the cream at the top, which now fetch high prices at antique stores. Newspaper reporters took no more notice than the rest of us.

Electric streetcars which rode on tracks were removed one line at a time until all were gone. Streetcar conductors were happy enough to move on to trolleys or buses. Other people scarcely noticed, except some of my brother's friends who enjoyed tormenting streetcar conductors.

Although boys often "pulled the trolley" on streetcar conductors during regular stops, this was too unimaginative for Fred's North Side buddies. They attacked near the Indiana State Fairgrounds streetcar turn-around.

A streetcar was two–directional. At the turn–around, the back end became the front end. So when the streetcar stopped and the conductor had moved the overhead electric feed–arm from one end of the streetcar to the other and the conductor had gone back inside to establish his seat at the opposite end of the streetcar, a boy would run behind the car and "pull the trolley," yanking the control line off the electric feed. While the conductor was busy returning the feed bar to the overhead line, another boy would throw a switch so the streetcar would start down the wrong track in its turn-around process. After the conductor started down the wrong track, he had to stop, once again reverse the overhead feed–arm, walk to the rear of the car, and remove the back seat in order to access the streetcar's reverse mechanism. While he was doing this, another boy would again "pull the trolley" on him.

When did architects stop putting front porches on new houses, and why did they do away with these wonderful places? This was a major social-changing decision made within the confines of architects' offices without the benefit of public or voter input.

Where we lived, neighbors shared porch swings to catch up on neighborhood news. On a rainy day, there was no better place for kids to play. On Saturday and Sunday mornings, men and women read the morning paper on front porches while drinking a second or third cup of coffee.

But new neighborhoods had no front porches. And neighbors found it hard to get to know one another. It was said that people had changed, that they had become cool and unfriendly. Architects escaped the blame they deserved.

Other trappings of our lives changed or disappeared, and I don't know why. Why didn't all children (adults for that matter) continue to drink delicious, chocolaty flavored Ovaltine? How severely was our creativity crippled when radio drama no longer was available to drive our imaginations? What happened to penny candy and nickel ice–cream cones? What became of community sings? And how many people can still sing *"Pack up your troubles in your old kit bag and smile, smile, smile."*?

And why, oh why, did circuses stop unfurling their tents within the neighborhoods of just about every girl and boy?

Willard Park was less than a half mile from the house we had moved from on State Street and not much farther from our Ohio Street house.

The park had a swimming pool but was flat and almost treeless. It also was close to a railroad siding and was a popular site for circuses and carnivals. After moving to the Ohio Street house, I missed the circus parades that had gone right past our State Street house. What a sight! Elephants paraded trunk to tail, and clowns blustered about shooting each other with squirt guns, walking tiny dogs and carrying bouquets of feather flowers.

There were people on stilts, wild animals in rolling cages pulled by horses, beautiful ladies in costumes, and, of course, the ring master, removing his tall black hat and bowing grandly to women on each side of the street.

After one big parade, Mom had gotten enough money together for us all to attend the circus, with fifteen cents left over for cotton candy.

A few years later—maybe I was nine—I learned at school that a carnival had set up business for a week at Willard Park. So on the following Saturday, I retrieved fifty cents from my clown bank and headed to the park.

I walked around the carnival, trying to decide how to spend my money. I noticed a big high school guy walking with his girlfriend. He walked with a swagger, like he was up to any challenge, or thought that he was. He stepped up to demonstrate his strength and win a prize by swinging a huge wooden mallet in an attempt to ring the bell high overhead. To get ready, he stretched his arms over his head and twisted his waist as far to the back and to each side as he could reach.

Then he picked up the mallet, sucked in air, and swung the mallet with all his strength. The bell-ringer started up the post really well; then it slowed and stopped before gravity pulled it back down. Most of the disc had gotten into a blue zone with the words "nice try."

He looked angry. As they walked away, he told his girlfriend, "Those things are rigged."

I walked in their direction. They stopped at the next booth, and the guy paid a quarter for three baseballs. He'd qualify to win a nice prize if he could throw the balls and knock down a bunch of stuffed canvas cats that were stacked up as the target. The cats were lined up perfectly straight. The boyfriend wound up like a professional pitcher and mowed down the stacked cats. Overhead were a row of prizes, big stuffed animals of different colors.

"Which one do you want, honey?"

She selected a pink bear, kissed the guy on the cheek, and they moved on down the row of attractions.

When they left the man running the booth stacked up the cats. But this time the cats were not quite in line. A couple of high school guys walked up to take their chances. Both threw the baseballs just as accurately as the boyfriend, but each time some of the cats stayed standing. It got me to thinking.

I circled the carnival and returned to the cat booth to find the cats stacked perfectly straight.

"I'd like to try that, mister," I told the cat-stacking man.

I exchanged a quarter for three baseballs and knocked all the cats flat. I selected a blue bear and started around the carnival again. "Tell 'em where you won that bear, kid," the man shouted after me.

On the next swing by the booth, the cats were not properly stacked, so I walked on to look at a massively fat woman and a skinny tattooed man. They were standing with robes on in front of a red tent. The woman was chewing a mouthful of gum.

You had to pay money to get inside the tent where you could get a good look at them. I kept on walking.

The next theater–tent had big colored pictures of a goat with two heads, a huge snake that was starting to swallow a pig whole, as well as a picture of an ape named King Kong. The ape had sharp teeth with blood dripping from its mouth. It must have been a very strong ape because it was bending and breaking the bars of its cage.

I could get in to see all three for a quarter. I suspected they had recaptured the ape and put it in a much stronger cage. But I decided to give the cat-stacker another chance.

When I approached the cat booth, a bald-headed man was throwing at the cats. A blond-headed woman was watching. Two cats stayed standing when he was out of baseballs.

"Gosh, Oliver," the woman said. I thought the man seemed upset. But I was sure of it after he picked up his cigar and bit down hard on it, because he also bit his mouth. He threw the cigar and cussed a blue streak.

The woman gave me an ashamed look, like I shouldn't have to listen to such words. Then her look changed to disgust. I figured she caught sight of my bear.

When they left, the cats went up straight and pretty as you please. Those cats were sitting ducks. After I won another bear the man said, "Get lost, kid. You got your share."

The bears ended up as Christmas presents for my two little nieces.

Then her look changed to disgust.
I figured she caught sight of my bear.

As long as I could remember, Jammy went downtown to the movies with Mrs. Roobush every Monday afternoon. They would select the movie they most wanted to see, usually showing at the

Indiana Theatre, Lowes, or the Circle Theatre. But sometimes they went to Keiths or the Lyric Theatre, which carried first–run movies not selected by the three larger theaters.

But most importantly, after attending a matinee, they would visit Craig's for a hot fudge sundae.

My grandmother was critical of the personal lives of many movie stars. Of course, this did not prevent her from attending movies in which they played leading roles. She was critical both of men and women.

Nearly every time he was pictured in magazines and newspapers, Rudolph Valentino was with a different woman. Consequently, he attracted most of her criticism. But she was among the first in line whenever a new movie came out featuring the film idol. Valentino died at a young age because of a ruptured appendix.

People would have supposed someone in my grandmother's immediate family had died. She stayed in her room for long periods, emerging to cook the family meal which she herself only picked at, eating even less than normal. This story about Jammy and Valentino was passed along after I was old enough to appreciate it.

Jammy was fond of both Tony and Dick, my sisters' husbands. But she seemed to make over Tony more than anybody else she knew. Tony lived his first sixteen years in Italy, and with black hair and a swarthy complexion, I think his looks reminded her of the deceased Valentino.

Mrs. Roobush was a robust, hard-working woman. She continued to be employed as a domestic after Mr. Roobush retired from laying bricks. Her husband had been hard of hearing for years and Mrs. Roobush always spoke at full volume, even when Mr. Roobush was not present.

Their house, with its intricate brickwork, is the one I imagined on Wistful Vista whenever I heard *Fibber McGee and Molly* on the radio. Mr. and Mrs. Roobush owned a 1929 Model–A Ford roadster which they drove each year to visit a daughter in Florida. Mr. Roobush did all the driving.

Mrs. Roobush never learned to drive. Few women her age had learned how, leaving driving to menfolk. She took the streetcar to work and to join Jammy downtown for their Monday afternoon movie and sundae. Jammy walked downtown but joined Mrs. Roobush on the streetcar ride home.

My grandmother was critical of the
personal lives of many movie stars.

One afternoon, Mrs. Wills, our downstairs neighbor, hollered up the stairs that she had a phone
call for Jammy. Mom paid Mrs. Wills a dollar each

month so we could receive and place important calls.

It was Mrs. Roobush on the phone. She asked Jammy to visit that evening. After dinner, Jammy invited me to walk with her to the Roobush house in our old neighborhood. When we arrived, we saw that the Roobush's daughter was visiting from Florida. I also noticed that Mrs. Roobush's neck was badly swollen on one side.

Pointing to her neck right off she said, "This is cancer," in her loud voice as through a megaphone. "The doctor says it'll kill me in a month or two," she shouted. Judging from her manner, Mrs. Roobush might have been talking about the weather or a recent movie she and Jammy had seen.

My grandmother's little face contorted as sting formed behind her eyes. "But I thought it was just something that would go away. I didn't think it was anything serious," Jammy said. It was as though she believed she could have saved Mrs. Roobush's life if she had recognized the swelling as cancer and taken her to a doctor.

"I thought it would go away, too," Mrs. Roobush responded. "It doesn't hurt. But after it kept getting bigger, I went to the doctor. He says it's cancer!"

On our walk home, Jammy repeated several times that she hadn't thought the swelling in Mrs. Roobush's neck was anything to worry about. And now she was about to die. It was more than my grandmother could deal with. Mrs. Roobush died in about six weeks, leaving Jammy without a good friend except for Aunt Mattie, who lived in Baltimore.

"This world and then the next," she said even more often.

The smartest kid
in class

I almost forgot to tell about singing in the church choir. That started way back when I was only six. The choir sang at Christ Church on the Circle, which a few years later became a cathedral, the bishop's home church for the Episcopal Diocese of Indianapolis.

Since I couldn't read when I first joined, let alone decipher music, my biggest challenge was to carry the large, red hymnal during the processional without dropping it.

I was told many years later why I had been recruited to join the choir before learning to read. The choirmaster had a six-year-old grandson,

Jerry Caldwell, whom he wanted in the choir. But Jerry needed another six–year–old to walk with and lead the choir during the processional. Because Fred was in the choir, I was recruited. Jerry and I were to become good friends and to get into trouble together, probably because we had so much in common.

Led by an acolyte carrying a cross, the choir made its way two–abreast, through a side door, down one side of the church and then up the center aisle.

When I was an adult, my sister, Dorothy, told me that I was as apt to carry the hymnal upside down as not and that I never sang.

"Why don't you sing?" she remembered asking me, back when I was six.

"Because I can't read," I had responded.

"Why don't you move your mouth and act like you're singing?" she wondered.

"That would be cheating," was the answer she recalled.

I had been sent to Sunday school at a nearby Presbyterian church when we lived on State Street. But my family had always been Episcopalians. When she was in high school, Mom had attended St. Paul's on Illinois Street, catty-cornered across from the Fox burlesque theater. That's where my sisters were later married. At St. Paul's, that is.

We started attending Christ Church because of the boys' choir. (This choir of men and boys has now been going strong for more than 125 years). Christ Church was a fixture on the Circle long before the Soldiers and Sailors Monument was built in its center.

Indianapolis was originally laid out with streets leading from the Circle like spokes.

Some of the city's wealthiest people attended Christ Church, including Eli Lilly, board chairman of Eli Lilly & Co., a pharmaceutical company headquartered in Indianapolis.

Mr. and Mrs. Lilly arrived at church in a chauffeur-driven limousine. Although they looked as close to being royalty as anyone I ever saw, they didn't act snooty or as though they thought of themselves as better than other churchgoers. Mr. Lilly's contributions largely funded the church and helped pay monthly checks to each choir boy. These checks were a very big deal. They reimbursed us for streetcar fare and added a little extra. I opened a savings account at a downtown bank where I deposited each check.

The Lilly Endowment, also headquartered in Indianapolis, was created by the Lilly family, and for a time had the largest capital endowment in the country. Indianapolis, the whole state of Indiana, and the entire nation have greatly benefited from this generous endowment fund.

Now I think of this wonderful family when people unfairly criticize the pharmaceutical industry. Of course, I also think of the millions of lives the drug industry has saved, improved and prolonged through industry research.

Jammy had a well prescribed church-attendance practice:

"I'll go when the choir sings the 'Hallelujah Chorus,'" she said.

Her rule of thumb kept her away from church except for an occasional Christmas and Easter service and a rare performance of Handel's *Messiah*. She figured the church had the option of singing the "Hallelujah Chorus" every Sunday, if they really wanted her in church.

I saved most of my monthly $4.50 choir earnings for a bicycle. After I got the bicycle, I began saving for college.

I was nearly ten when the war ended. President Roosevelt had died not long before and Harry Truman, who had been our vice president, became President of the United States. He made the fateful decision to drop atomic bombs on Japan, forcing their surrender and finally ending that terrible war.

None of my friends' dads had been killed or wounded. I had not seen my own father for so long I couldn't even remember what he looked like. I didn't know it, but I was never to see him again.

Ernie Puckett was the smartest kid in my fifth–grade class. But you had to know him to realize it. I think he remembered everything he ever heard, and he could put ideas together.

Science was Ernie's best subject, and he was starting to be very good in arithmetic, too. When I had problems understanding a lesson, Ernie helped me. But he had problems of his own. And

I had no idea how to help him. Ernie was a terrible reader and spelling was like Greek to him.

Because Ernie was flunking spelling, he buckled down and worked harder than any kid I ever saw to bring up his grade. The hard work was paying off; he started getting 100s on his spelling tests. I saw his grades because he sat next to me.

One day Miss Morgan returned our most recent spelling test but saved Ernie's for last. She walked to his seat and slammed his paper down in front of him. A big red zero was marked at the top.

"You're nothing but a cheater," she shouted. "I reversed the order of the words in the test, but you wrote them in the order I assigned them for study. I've caught you red-handed."

"Ernie didn't cheat, Miss Morgan," I said. "If he had cheated I would have seen it," I told her because my seat was so close to his.

"You keep out of this," she said to me. "You probably helped him cheat."

Ernie was mortified. He didn't speak. Then he hid his face into folded arms on his desktop. His shoulders sort of quivered, but he didn't make a sound.

As long as I knew him, Ernie couldn't spell and could hardly read. After being humiliated by Miss Morgan, he became a boy I no longer knew. He kept to himself and didn't even participate in games unless one of us made it a point to recruit him. During spelling tests, Ernie simply closed his eyes and turned his paper in empty.

Year after year Ernie attended school, but he wasn't really there. He dropped out when he turned sixteen I heard.

When I was an adult, I concluded that the smartest person in my classes at School 14 was not a cheater but dyslexic. How terrible it must have been for Ernie to realize people thought he was stupid—maybe he even thought of himself in the same way! But with the right kind of help, he could have gotten beyond his learning disability.

How hard he must have worked to memorize the letters in the right sequence for spelling tests only to be accused of cheating. How many children must have suffered a similar fate before educators learned to recognize this common disability and help kids to overcome it?

We had periodic fire drills at School 14. After the war was finally over, we added a new drill. Fire drills continued, but we also began the practice of preparing for a Communist atomic bomb attack by crouching under our desks. We didn't think being under our desks would save us from a nearby atom bomb explosion, but maybe flying window glass would miss us if the bombs were far enough away.

And so we traded in our fear of German or Japanese attack for a far worse fear—that of an atomic bomb attack by the Russians.

Teachers' comments on my own report cards chronicled my laziness and my slow advancement through the grades:

"Donald doesn't apply himself." (Miss Spencer)

"He could do much better if he would only try." (Miss McMann)

"A window gazer." (Miss Laudermilk)

"A lazy pupil." (Miss Ruehrschecht)

Miss Morgan added "smart aleck" to my list of faults:

"Donald is a smart aleck. You should wash his mouth out with soap." Which is what Mom did.

Miss Morgan had instructed our class to find out the population of Indianapolis. I had not given the assignment another thought until the next day when out of the blue Miss Morgan said:

"Donald! Stand up. Now tell the class how many people there are in the city of Indianapolis."

"I don't know, Miss Morgan. I haven't gotten around to counting them yet."

The class started to laugh...until Miss Morgan's icy stare shut them up.

"If any pupil had given such a smart aleck answer when I was in school, he would have been severely disciplined. Your parents will hear of this. If you ever try to use a smart mouth around me again, you will go to Mr. Thornburg's office. Do you understand?"

"Yes ma'am." She was coming in loud and clear. Luckily, I didn't actually say, "You're coming in loud and clear."

Living to tell
about it

During those years, I had many heroes besides Dr. Abdon, my bronze–star–winning dentist. And not a single hero let me down.

Some were to be found across the street from West Bakery at the Strand Theater on Saturday afternoon. For twenty–five cents a kid could eat popcorn, watch two movies, three cartoons and a newsreel, learn about coming attractions, and most importantly catch up on the Tom Mix serial.

The bad guys always had the upper hand just before we were warned not to miss next week's thrilling episode.

The prettiest young woman anyone had ever seen would be tied to a railroad track with the onrushing train just a few feet away. Then the *"Continued next week"* line would come on the screen with a verbal promotion of the upcoming installment.

The following week Tom Mix, a cowboy hero who always outsmarted the bad guys, would ride up in a cloud of dust just in time to cut the pretty young lady free. Somehow, the train was always much farther away the second week than I had remembered it being the week before.

...From out of the past come the thundering hoofbeats of the great horse, Silver. The Lone Ranger rides again!

On the radio, I always listened to *The Lone Ranger* after school and before supper every summer afternoon. He was my number one radio hero. And why not? *The William Tell Overture* would play and then fade real low so you'd hear that:

"...*Nowhere in the pages of history can one find a greater champion of justice. Return with us now to those thrilling days of yesteryear. From out of the past come the thundering hoofbeats of the great horse, Silver. The Lone Ranger rides again!*"

Singing cowboys became popular at the movies. Gene Autry was the first such film idol. Later, Roy Rogers, who I learned had grown up in Cincinnati, came on the scene with the beautiful Dale Evans. Once, I actually touched Roy Rogers' outstretched hand, as did several hundred other kids at Victory Field. He was riding the famous horse, Trigger. Talk about a pretty horse!

Victory Field was home to the Indianapolis Indians baseball team, which, when I was a kid, was the Triple-A farm club for the Pittsburgh Pirates and then the Cleveland Indians. Victory Field was later renamed Bush Stadium in honor of Owen J. Bush. Many years later, a new ball field opened near downtown Indianapolis and was again named Victory Field. Bush was a longtime

Detroit Tiger. When his playing days were over, he acquired interests in the Indianapolis Indians.

But most importantly, he had grown up next door to where my grandmother had lived at the time. "He was a wonderful person and always so good to his mother," Jammy recalled.

My Indians won the American Association pennant in 1948 with a roster of heroes. I listened to every game on the radio. However, I did get to see a few games in person. In 1948 the Indians beat out the Milwaukee Brewers, the Saint Paul Saints, the Kansas City Blues, the Toledo Mud Hens, the Louisville Colonels, the Columbus Red Birds and the Minneapolis Millers, though not in that order.

The team was managed by the great Al Lopez, who went on to manage the Cleveland Indians, taking them to the World Series. He'd been a catcher during his ball–playing days. And he was one classy catcher! While in Indianapolis he sometimes caught the second game of double-headers.

I saw one such game. With runners on first and third, the first base runner attempted to steal second. Lopez threw out the guy on third who was watching to see if his teammate would be safe at second.

Tom Saffel, Ted Beard and Pete Castiglione are the players I remember most from that team. Saffel and Beard were outfielders, Castiglione the shortstop. All three lived in a rooming house on Michigan Street, across from Tech High School, not far from my home. My buddies and I talked to them a couple of times and we got their autographs.

I've always considered Ted Beard the best baseball player who never made it big in the majors. It's doubtful any right fielder ever had a better arm. Beard routinely threw strikes to third and home when runners tried to push their luck. He was greased lightning on the bases or chasing flies. Beard was almost certain to steal second whenever he got on first, and he often stole third as well. He was a pretty good hitter too, hitting close to 300 for the Indians.

*My Indians won the American Association
pennant in 1948 with a roster of heroes.*

The Pirates brought him up and you would have thought he was Babe Ruth, hitting home runs in consecutive games, until the word got around that Beard couldn't hit a curve. Then he was returned to Indianapolis, until the following year when he was again called up to the same sequence of events. Pitchers have short memories.

Old Forbes Field in Pittsburgh had markers to record the longest home runs ever hit in that grand old ballpark. Ted Beard's name was out there with the mightiest of major league greats. In fact, his nickname was "Little Mighty." He ultimately managed the Indianapolis Indians and also proved himself to be an excellent manager.

When I was eleven, I had finally saved enough to buy a bicycle. Now I could ride over to see my State Street buddies, visiting Dick Leary and Benny Jones after school and during the summer.

Dick was a Boy Scout with Troop 41 at Trinity Lutheran School. So Dick invited me to join, and Benny soon joined, as well.

I worked hard and earned my Tenderfoot badge. Then I worked toward becoming a Second-Class Scout. Early in November our Scoutmaster, Mr. Briggs, arranged for a weekend camping trip to Camp Rotary near Crawfordsville. We would leave Saturday morning and return home Sunday afternoon.

I was to have my tonsils removed the following Saturday. Mom was afraid I might catch a cold and the operation would have to be postponed. After I promised to stay warm and dry and Mr. Briggs told her he would keep a close eye on me, we climbed aboard a school bus and headed out.

It had rained a lot that fall. And that week it turned cold and snowed real hard. The camp was hilly and heavily wooded. We were assigned a large cabin and we each selected a bunk. While Mr. Briggs was building a fire in the fireplace to heat the place up, some of us decided to look around outside.

Bob Gordon, who like Dick was thirteen or fourteen, joined Dick, Benny and me. First we climbed down a snow–covered hill and then followed a small tributary stream. It had turned into a perfect blue–sky day, sunny and in the low 20s.

This was the day I almost died.

The snow from the night before was the kind that falls soft on each twig and branch and stays. Because there was no wind and it got colder, the snow continued to rest where it had fallen to create patterns of bright lace in the sunshine.

"Look at these snowflakes," Dick told us. "Out of a trillion-trillion snowflakes, no two are alike." We looked and couldn't see any two that looked alike. I'd never paid any attention to snowflakes.

Bob Gordon was a big kid, one of those people who always seemed to be smiling. He sang us a song about a little brown jug: *"Little brown jug was in my arm. Off I went to the country farm. Stubbed my toe and down I fell and broke that little brown jug to… … …welllll."* We staggered with laughter.

Then Dick took his turn. To the tune of *"Twinkle, Twinkle, Little Star,"* he sang:

"Starkle, starkle, little twink, who in the heck you are I think. Up above me oh so low, I'm a better man than you are, Ol' Black Joe." We all laughed at Dick too, who was as unaware of the racial slur as we were.

We wore galoshes over our shoes and enjoyed crashing through the shallow little stream, where underfoot the ice shattered like window glass. We examined pieces of the ice, the underside revealing a tiny crystalline world of stalactites and out-branching diamonds that glittered in the sun.

We called all streams "creeks" and wondered aloud why the word wasn't spelled, c-r-i-c-k.

And then we practiced our Scouting repertoire:

"A Scout is trustworthy, loyal, helpful, friendly, courteous, kind, obedient, cheerful, thrifty, brave, clean and reverent."

"On my honor, I will do my best to do my duty to God and my country and to obey the Scout law; to help other people at all times; to keep myself physically strong, mentally awake and morally straight."

We saw where animals had come to the stream to drink. There were deer tracks and some small clawed prints we guessed to be raccoon or fox.

We had worked our way to where the little stream flowed into Sugar Creek. Here we turned left, moving in the same direction as the current which, because of the heavy rain and snow in recent weeks, had become an angry river. No ice had formed on the swift–flowing water, though the banks were crusted with ice.

It was a wild area, but getting back to camp would be a simple matter of retracing our foot-prints in the snow. Nearly two hours had elapsed since we'd ambled away from the camp, but returning before dark didn't worry us. That Mr. Briggs had no idea where we were and might be concerned never entered our minds.

We were walking four abreast, Benny closest to the trees, then Dick, Bob and me. Bob was teach-ing us the words to his little brown jug song.

My world flew out from under me with my feet.

I slid feet first, on my belly, down the icy bank toward the angry water. My fingers clawed at the crusted ice beside the river and caught on a crack. Only my galoshes–covered feet went into the water.

I don't think I hollered. I didn't need to.

Benny grabbed a tree limb and one of Dick's ankles who also held onto Bob by his ankles. Bob threw off his gloves and stretched down toward me. Using both hands, he grabbed my wrists instead of my wool-gloved hands, and shouted at me to hold his wrists as well. Then he pulled. How the guys were smart enough to know what to do, I couldn't imagine.

Ever so slowly I inched up the slick slope, trying to use my knees and feet for traction but with little success. Finally, I got a toehold on that blessed crack that my fingers had snagged earlier.

A pull from Bob and a leg push from me and I was safe!

I may have been only eleven, but I realized how close death had come to me. It was birthday, Christmas and Easter rolled into one for me.

Electricity flowed in my veins and I couldn't stop talking. I shook Bob's hand, then Dick's and Benny's too. Then I slapped each of their backs.

"You deserve a lifesaving merit badge!" I told Bob. "You too, Dick! And Benny! You all deserve lifesaving merit badges!" They were pretty pleased with themselves as well.

Dick said we should return to camp, so we headed back, single file, carefully hugging the tree line along Sugar Creek.

I inched up the slick slope, trying to use my knees and feet for traction but with little success.

Except for wet gloves and damp trousers, we had stayed pretty dry, thanks mostly to our galoshes. We turned into the little stream and easily followed where we'd crashed and splashed through the thin ice and shallow water.

The sun was nearly out of sight, but with the half–light of dusk, we had no trouble finding our snowy footprints at the base of the hill below the camp, where we had first come down the wooded ravine to follow the stream.

We burst into the cabin's kitchen full of life to find Mr. Briggs peeling a mountain of potatoes, which were to become fried potatoes. I also noticed a large mound of onions. He had not worried about us much at first, but after nearly three hours he was very upset.

We proudly regaled him with all of our stories, especially how they'd saved my life. But nothing we said pleased him in the least. Mr. Briggs was born in Wales. He valued high moral living and rules to help young people hew the straight and narrow.

He told us that Jesus died on the cross to save us from sin, but that meant we had an obligation to cause Him as little additional heartache as possible. And today we had let Him down.

Then he told me I had also let my mother down, because I was supposed to be avoiding catching a cold instead of splashing around in icy creeks.

"Suppose you had drowned. Can you imagine how terrible I'd feel having to tell your mother after promising to take special care of you?"

I wasn't feeling so great anymore.

Mr. Briggs gave us kitchen duty peeling and slicing the rest of the potatoes and chopping the onions. He also told us we were to wash all of the dishes as well, after everyone had eaten.

While we were hiking, Mr. Briggs must have bought all the onions within twenty miles. Fried potatoes have never been cried over so much.

After dinner, each patrol was to dream up and give a skit with the prize of ice cream for the winners. Dick had our skit in mind. We talked about it while washing the dishes.

"Benny and Joe will be horses, okay? Bob, you're a farmer who owns one of the horses and I'm the farmer who owns the other horse. Schroeder, you will be the big, smart, city slicker.

"Now what happens is this: we keep getting our horses mixed up. We can't tell them apart. So I cut an ear off my horse. But the next time I see Bob's horse, he's cut the same ear off. Next, I cut the other ear off, only to find that Bob's cut the other ear off his horse, too. Next it's the tail, with the same result. So we start arguing and getting mad at each other.

"That's when you come along Don, the big, smart, city slicker. Now you say, 'Hold on, what's the trouble here?' Then we tell you. And you say, 'Well, let's see here.' Then you pull out a string and you measure the horses. And you say, 'Sure enough the white horse is an inch taller than the black one.'"

So we ran through it and got it down good.

Our patrol was the last to perform. The other skits were plenty good, especially one by a patrol of older guys. But Dick was confident we'd win.

Our skit went something like this:

Dick to Bob: "We sure are having trouble keeping these horses straight. It's a real problem. They look just alike."

Bob to Dick: "You're right. Well, I'll see you later." (Both Dick and Bob lead horses off stage and then return.)

Dick to Bob: "I solved our problem. I cut the right ear off my horse. Now we can tell them apart."

Bob to Dick: "Oh, no. I cut the right ear off my horse, too. We still have the same problem. Well, I'll see you later. (Both Dick and Bob lead horses off stage and then return.)

Dick to Bob: "I went home and cut the other ear off my horse."

Bob to Dick: "Please don't tell me that, because I did the very same thing. This is sure a problem." (Both Dick and Bob lead horses off stage and then return.)

Bob to Dick: "I fixed our problem. I cut the tail off my horse. Now we'll know 'em apart."

Dick to Bob: "You jerk! I cut the tail off my horse, too! Now we'll never be able to tell them apart." (Enter me, the big, smart, city slicker).

Me to them: "Here, here! What seems to be the problem?"

Dick: "We couldn't tell our horses apart. So I cut one ear off mine. Then Farmer Brown, here, he cuts the same ear off his horse. Then I cut off the other ear. Then he does the same thing. Then it's the tails. Now we have no idea how we'll ever keep these horses straight."

Me: "I think I can solve this little problem if you will be kind enough to give me a minute," I say, pulling out my handy–dandy string and measuring Benny horse and then Joe horse.

Me: "Sure enough, one horse is an inch bigger than the other one."

For what seemed like a long time, everybody just looked at me. The crowd sure wasn't laughing, either. Then Dick shouted:

"Schroeder—you idiot."

Before I knew what was happening, I was being punched to the ground by angry farmers and horses. Our skit finished dead last.

The winning skit had guys running one at a time onto the makeshift stage. In turn, each shouted: "The viper is coming!" "The viper is coming!" After six or eight such warnings, a boy showed up carrying a large rag. He announced: "I am the viper!" Then he asked: "Vhere are the vindows you vant me to vipe?"

I had to agree with Dick, Bob and Benny that our skit would have won if the big, smart, city slicker hadn't flubbed the punch line. And of course I learned why they call it "the punch line."

Sure enough, one horse is an inch bigger than the other one.

The fireplace burned out that night, and I woke up shivering. All the bunks were shoved together, and Dick's was right next to mine.

"Hey, Dick! Are you awake?"

"Yeah."

"I sure am cold. Aren't you?"

"Naw, Mom packs more blankets than I need. Pull the top one off for yourself."

I got warm but couldn't go back to sleep thinking about the day. Then I heard Dick. He was shivering, and it was as though he was trying his best not to be heard. I took his blanket and arranged it partly over him and partly over me. Soon I was asleep.

The next day was Sunday. At a makeshift church service, Mr. Briggs gave a prayer that included thanks to God for saving me and for using Benny, Dick and Bob to pull me out of the river.

I was glad for the prayer but sorry I hadn't given God any credit for my rescue nor even thanked Him!

After some hotdogs, we headed home.

I had survived the camping trip after all without catching a cold. So the guys kindly devoted the bus ride to preparing me for my operation.

"We don't want you to worry about having your tonsils out," said Dick. "But it helps if you know what to expect.

"It's no big deal, really. What they do is they strap you down on this table that has wheels. Then they push you into the operating room. Then this real ugly nurse comes at you with a handkerchief soaked in ether.

"She puts it over your nose and mouth and orders you to breathe and to start counting backwards from ten to one.

"About the time you get to seven, funny green patterns show up in front of your eyeballs. You're mostly passed out, but you sort of know that people are around.

"Then you black out. That is, if you're lucky. Sometimes the nurse doesn't give you enough ether, and you look blacked out but you're not exactly. If you're not totally out, you can feel them putting this contraption into your mouth. They crank it and crank it to open your mouth real wide because the surgeon probably has huge meat hooks for hands and he needs to get them in there.

"Then the surgeon arrives and he's all covered with blood from cutting people open all day. He grabs his knife, spits on it and sharpens it a little bit. Then he gets most of his face into your mouth so he can see what he's doing and starts to cut away at your tonsils.

"Doctors always cut out a lot more than they need to. That's because they don't want your mom coming back to complain and say they missed part of your tonsils.

"By this time you're bleeding like a stuck pig. If the ugly nurse remembers to sop it up, you won't drown in your own blood. But don't worry; people hardly ever drown in their own blood.

"Then they stick these really long pliers back through your mouth and up into where the hole in your throat is, the hole where your snot drains into your stomach. The pliers have a right angle in them, so they can get up into the inside of your nose and grab your adenoids.

"Adenoids are slimy things. So they're hard to hold onto. It will probably take six or eight tries before they get hold of them. But once they grab them good, they pluck right out of there like oysters: first one, then the next!"

Bob made a sucking noise and finished with a *"plop."* He did it twice, one for each adenoid, I supposed.

"But remember," Dick continued," most guys are knocked out cold, and they don't know any of this stuff is happening to them. So it's nothing to worry about."

Then Bob took over:

"Pretty soon you'll wake up in what they call the recovery room. And you're coughing up blood. And you upchuck like crazy from the ether and your throat hurts like fire where they cut out your tonsils, and your puke is all over the wounds."

"And that ugly nurse is there," Dick added.

"And she's really mad at you, like it's your fault you're barfing from the ether, when she was the one who held it over your nose too long.

"And you wonder where your mom is. And nobody tells you that they won't let her in until you look a whole lot better and they clean you up good. Because if she sees you throwing up blood, they figure she won't pay them. So you may not see her for a couple of days."

"About that time," Bob added, "you'll start wishing I'd let you drown in the river."

Then Dick said: "Yeah, you will, Schroeder. But don't worry. Most guys live through this ordeal. The chances are good you'll live to tell us all about it."

What I remember from the operation was that the nurses weren't mean or ugly, but nice.

They were nuns who staffed St. Vincent's, a Catholic hospital. After the operation, one nurse kept rushing into my room to tell me that Johnny Lujack had passed for yet another Notre Dame touchdown.

A radio was playing at the nurses' station. Notre Dame was easily winning the game. And the nurse was so happy it was contagious.

Nakedness

On Scout Sunday, I attended church with Troop 41 at Trinity Lutheran Church, near the downtown area on Ohio Street. Mr. Briggs asked me if I understood the service okay.

I told him that I didn't notice much that was different from the Episcopal service. The Lutheran minister seemed to talk about sin instead of sins. And in the creed, a belief was proclaimed in the Christian Church instead of in the Catholic Church. Catholic means universal, I had been told, not simply Roman Catholic.

Holy Cross Catholic Church and School was a block east of School 14 on Ohio Street. Lots of

Catholic kids lived in our neighborhood. After grade school, most of the kids from Holy Cross went on to attend Sacred Heart, St. Mary's or Cathedral high schools. Other kids from area neighborhoods went to Tech High School.

In the years I was growing up, there was considerable prejudice against Catholics.

When I was in junior high, a Holy Cross eighth grader forced a buddy of mine to the ground. With a pocket knife to his neck, he inquired, "You like Catholics, don't you?" My friend told him, "I sure do!"

I don't know about my friend, but I liked all the Catholics I knew. I was simply prejudiced against their Church—one of those mindless feelings. Mindless feelings pretty well describes prejudice. I also was guilty of the same mindless feelings toward others. But I sure couldn't explain why.

A sermon's summary casts a spotlight on prejudice: God loves people against whom you are prejudiced as much as He loves you. Think how you'll feel when you get to Heaven and run into these people.

There was more racial prejudice in those days than today. A few black kids (we called them colored kids at the time) went to School 14. None of them were in my class. And I didn't know any of them but I got to be pretty good friends with several black kids in high school. Other than skin color, they were like everybody else I knew, except some were from families even poorer than mine.

The summer after I got my tonsils out, our Scout troop went to Camp Belzer for a week. The camp was located on the northeast edge of Indianapolis. It was so close that Mr. Briggs could work during the day and be with us at night.

Sometimes a kid needs to be taken down a few notches. I suppose I did.

Some of the older guys had tried the ancient snipe-hunting routine with me, but I knew all about it, so I didn't fall for it. They had wanted to get me out in the woods with me holding a burlap bag to catch the fictitious snipes. Then they planned to hide and watch me. They wanted me to get scared and maybe even cry. They then hoped to show up and laugh at me for being so stupid as to believe that a snipe was an actual animal that would voluntarily jump into a burlap bag.

But I laughed at them instead and would have no part of it. They also tried a few other tricks, but I was on guard against each and enjoyed being able to frustrate them.

One afternoon shortly before dinner, I was lying on my bunk reading a comic book after attending a class about Indians. I heard some guys coming my way, but I didn't pay any attention. They were always coming or going.

When they stepped into the tent and tried to act all casual, I knew something was up. There were about five of them, all friends of mine, but older. The next thing I knew, they were grabbing at my trousers. Realizing they were trying to take my pants off, I started swinging at them and fighting with every ounce of energy I could muster.

None of it made any sense because I undressed with other guys when we changed for swimming and thought nothing of it. But now I fought them like a demon. One of them got a bloody lip for his effort and I whacked a couple of others pretty good too.

After what seemed like a long struggle, they managed to pull my trousers off and it was over.

I didn't know what to do or say so I just lay there on the bunk, out of breath from the fight, while they stood around and looked at me. The show wasn't close to being worth the admission price.

What I really felt like was naked. What made me feel that way wasn't just that I didn't have anything on. It was that they were all looking at me. It was sort of like saying a stupid thing in class and everybody getting a good peek at my ignorance.

The guys seemed really quiet. Maybe they were as embarrassed as I was. Then they all left, like they were following some offstage cue.

I hadn't yet crossed that divide between child and would-be adult. I had no idea about the worries of that crossing, the cross–currents of emotion and responsibility it thrusts our way, or how it ends childhood.

Dick hadn't been involved, but he told me he knew what was planned.

When I asked him why they did it, he said I had a smart mouth and the guys wanted to cut me down to size a little bit. Dick said I'd fought like crazy and didn't cry or anything. He figured they were still frustrated because I hadn't acted the way they wanted me to.

"Don't you know how mad you make people sometimes?" he asked. I told him that I didn't.

"Well, you did it again today," he said. "In that class about Indians, the Eagle Scout who was teaching asked where American Indians originated. And there were a couple–dozen guys in the class. Three or four raised their hands. And you were one of them.

"So he called on Bob Gordon. And Bob said he figured Indians have always been here. And that wasn't the answer he was looking for, so he called on Jack Martin. And Jack said Indians came to this country from India in birchbark canoes.

"And that's the wrong answer, and then he called on you.

"And you say that thousands of years ago, when the glaciers were at just their perfect phase in the melting cycle, that Asian hunters, who were the forefathers of the people who eventually were to be called Indians, came across some sort of land bridge between Siberia and Alaska. They were in search of wild game. They followed the game south along the Pacific Ocean. Some went all the way down to Central and South America. But others fanned out into the North American continent.

"Then you say the American Indians are descendants of Mongolians. And you end by turning to Jack and telling him that Columbus called the people he found in the New World 'Indians' because he thought he had landed in India.

"Can you imagine how that made Jack feel? And what about Bob! They're a couple of years older than you and you made them look like jerks. And you know what else? The guy who was teaching didn't like it either, because he was going to cover all that stuff in his class. And you had already said it all.

"And you wonder why they pulled your pants off!"

Dick made me mad, but I could see that he was right. And that made it even worse.

"That Eagle Scout who was teaching asked where Indians came from and I'd read about Indians. So I told him. He shouldn't have asked the question if he didn't want someone to answer it." I walked out and went somewhere to be by myself.

I shared a tent with Dick and Benny. Once we were talking and I was sitting on my bunk and Benny was sitting cross-legged on the ground, intent on what Dick was saying.

"Here, Benny," I said, "hold my foot." Benny took the foot I held up and cradled it for me like a footstool as he listened to Dick. After twenty or thirty seconds, Benny realized he'd been pretty stupid, dropped my foot and said, "What am I doing this for?" Then I laughed and he did too.

But Dick didn't laugh.

"See. Now you've made Ben look stupid. How do you suppose that makes him feel?" he asked.

We talked a lot that week because we had plenty of time on our hands.

Dick and Benny's grandmother had died over the previous year and I knew they missed her. She was a wonderful person.

Once we talked about her and I said, "She really was a good woman. She must be in Heaven."

"Of course she's in Heaven," Dick said angrily.

"Why are you mad at me now?" I wanted to know.

"Don't you learn anything in church and Sunday school?" Dick asked.

Benny took the foot I held up and
cradled it for me like a footstool.

"Sure."

"No you don't, or you wouldn't say such an idiotic thing about her being good so she must be in Heaven."

What he said really ticked me off because I was just trying my best to be nice.

Dick was leaning back on a camp stool, giving me a mean look. I got up, shoved him and sent him sprawling, then walked out of the tent. He really got my goat.

"Somebody needs to whip you good!" he shouted.

Dick's comment about me not learning anything in Sunday school and in church was close to being on target. I didn't pay much attention to the church service or to sermons.

And in those days, boys in the choir didn't have Sunday school. Instead of knowing that Jesus paid the full price for our sins and opened our way into Heaven, I thought it was up to me to be good and to stop sinning. I hoped I'd be good enough so that when I died, Jesus would go to bat for me.

On stage
and screen

During choir practice at Christ Church one summer afternoon, we learned we were to be in a
movie called *Johnny Holiday* that was to be filmed
in Plainfield, just west of Indianapolis, at the
youth reformatory.

The movie was about a boy who had gotten
in with the wrong crowd and was sent to reform
school. A reform school employee, played by
William Bendix, helps the boy return to a use-
ful, law-abiding life. The reform school is visited
at Christmas time by Hoosier songwriter Hoagy
Carmichael who introduces a new song, "My
Christmas Song for You." Indiana's governor was

in the movie too—Gov. Henry Shricker. He was known for the big white hat he always wore or carried.

We were to sing *"My Christmas Song for You"* while trying to look like inmates at the Indiana Boys School.

The majority of the movie was filmed at the Plainfield reform school. Our scene took place in the auditorium. Seated at a piano on the stage, Hoagy Carmichael invited the inmates (us choir boys and a few inmates) to join him on the stage and sing the song. As if by magic, we knew the words:

"My Christmas song for you is all the old things tried and true. A window bright with candle light to set your heart aglow. Through the door a Christmas tree sparkling with dreams made for me and you. Wishing I was there, sweetheart, to share all of the season's blessings."

One guy who crowded around Mr. Carmichael's piano was Stanley Clements, an original Dead End Kid, from the long series of *Dead End Kids* movies. He was the one who took the goofy guy's cap and whacked him on the head with it in every *Dead End Kids* movie. By this time he was into his thirties and doing his best to look like a mean teenager. The director wanted him and my brother to get into a pushing match, jostling for position around the piano.

After several unsuccessful takes, the director abandoned the pushing scene. Clements was good at looking mean (if not like a teenager) and Fred was good at looking like a teenager (if not at looking mean). While Clements' movie career continued, my brother's came to an abrupt end.

Every choir boy got $25 for being in the movie. The world premiere of *Johnny Holiday* was held at the Lyric Theatre in downtown Indianapolis. Searchlights were brought in to scan the sky in front of the theater. The great Bob Hope was the master of ceremonies, and to start things off the choir went out on stage to sing the National Anthem.

Backstage prior to the show, Mr. Hope told three pretty young women exactly what to say during a comedy skit. He put it all together on the spot. And the skit came off as though everybody had practiced for many hours.

Gov. Henry Shricker, the Indiana governor known for his white hat, gets a salute from William Bendix.

The following year, a dozen guys from the choir also sang in what was known as the "Starlight Musicals." This involved several productions over the summer. We had a small part in the opera, *Carmen*. It was performed at "The Butler Bowl," which had a huge stage placed in front of the horseshoe end of the Butler University football stadium.

We carried toy rifles. And playing like soldiers, we marched and sang a song in front of a cigarette factory.

As near as I could figure out, we were sort of mocking real Spanish soldiers who were also on the stage watching us. For our work, each boy earned a silver dollar.

Even worse
nakedness

I received my formal sex education in junior high. By this time, classes moved between bells to different classrooms, subjects and teachers.

Miss Garrett taught the section which was more than just sex education—actually a study tour of our entire bodies. Both boys and girls made up the class.

We spent quite a long time on our brains and nervous systems. Study time was devoted pretty equally to the heart and circulatory system, our digestive system, our skeletal system, our nerves, muscles and so forth. Even our skin and hair came in for examination.

As the end of the term approached, several of the guys wondered outside of her hearing whether Miss Garrett would have enough time for the sex part.

It turned out she had as much time as she wanted—actually a bit more than she wanted. On the final day, after spending most of the time reviewing lungs, she said, "The final organ in the body is the reproductive system...which is located in a well-protected place."

Her timing was less than perfect. With at least a minute before the class bell was to ring, there was ample time for kids to snicker and for Miss Garrett's face to turn the color of beets in vinegar.

As long as I could remember, it had been a foregone conclusion that my brother and I would attend college. Mom assumed we would go and that it would mostly be our responsibility to come up with the money. (With my grades, a scholarship wasn't possible).

There was never any discussion about "if" we got to college. It all had to do with "when" we got to college. The fact that kids who came out of School 14 didn't go to college and often didn't finish high school had no bearing on the matter.

Most of our earnings from the church choir went into individual college savings accounts. Fred also got some pretty good jobs. But I could find only a few odd jobs to earn money for college.

I dragged an old push lawn mower from house to house, looking for grass-cutting jobs but didn't have much success because people in our neighborhood cut their own instead of paying somebody to do it for them.

My first real job was selling ice cream. The summer before junior high, I pushed a heavy ice cream cart around Indianapolis' East Side just about every day it didn't rain. Eskimo pies, ice cream cups and sandwiches, fudgies, drumsticks, different flavored popsicles—I had the entire line. A full load would net $4.75 for me if I sold out, which I did every time I went out.

My face and arms turned from white to red to brown, but my muscles showed no inclination toward getting any bigger. In those days, I admired the ninety–seven-pound weakling, advertising for Charles Atlas, who got sand kicked into his face on the back cover of every comic book. I was just an eighty–seven-pound weakling myself.

I headed east from the ice cream company near downtown Indianapolis. Ringing the bells to attract attention, I pushed the cart up one north and south–running street and down the next one, between New York and Michigan streets, all the way to Ellenberger Park and then back until the cart was empty.

It was not a route that reflected good business judgment on my part, because few children of poor parents bought any ice cream. I would have been better off bypassing the poor neighbor-hoods entirely. But in the end, I always managed to sell all my ice cream.

By the time school started, my weight had shot up from eighty–seven to eighty–nine pounds. A good friend who was close to my age had spent much of his summer stretched out on a davenport, reading comic books and drinking cokes. (We never said "soda" unless we visited a soda fountain to order a tall cone-shaped glass with ice cream, soda water and flavorings. Sorry,

Coca-Cola, nobody told us we were violating your trademark.)

My friend's favorite kind of coke was Pepsi! Over the summer, he grew three inches, gained twenty pounds and added muscles like a weight lifter.

If Thomas Jefferson had seen the two of us, he never would have claimed that "all men are created equal."

The next summer, I got a job riding my bicycle delivering blue prints and Photostats for the Lieber store on North Capitol in the near-downtown area. Liebers sold architectural supplies there as well and had a second downtown store which did framing, had an art gallery and sold art supplies

Those were the days before automobile air conditioning. Every car window was rolled down on hot days. I had the uncanny knack of riding by a line of cars stopped for a traffic light when some guy would spit tobacco or other mouth juices just in time to hit me. Jerry Caldwell from church had the same job that I had and with the same slimy result. Hardly a week went by that it didn't happen to us.

Water coolers could be found in most of the offices I visited with deliveries. Salt tablet dispensers were mounted next to many coolers. And my supervisor encouraged delivery boys to take salt tablets, especially on very hot days.

Once, when the temperature flirted with one hundred degrees, I decided to follow my supervisor's instructions. Under the theory that more is better, I downed six or eight salt pills. After riding my bike just a few blocks, I became so ill I went to the sidewalk and sort of collapsed. A businessman tried to help me. But I had no suggestion on what he could do. I involuntarily helped myself by regurgitating most of the salt.

One day I left Liebers to deliver a blueprint only to discover that my bicycle had been stolen. I filled out a theft report with the Indianapolis Police Department and bought a used bike so that I could continue working.

A month or so later, I was making a delivery when I saw three guys who were about my age riding bikes. One was on my old bike. There was no mistaking that it was my bike, even though the fenders had been removed. It had the same old crooked seat and the same paint job. A kid knows his bike like a cowboy knows his horse. I overtook the trio, grabbed my bike by the handle bars and said to the kid who was riding it:

"This is my bike and you stole it!"

"What do you think you're going to do about it?" the kid inquired. (Where's a policeman when you need one? Right across the street, thank you very much!)

"If you don't get off my bike right now, I'm going to call that cop, and you'll find yourself in reform school!" I responded.

I figured my answer must have been the right one, because the kid jumped off my bike, sat on the crossbars of a buddy's bike and said, "Let's get out of here."

So I sold my old bike for what I'd paid for the second bicycle, which had fenders and a better seat. And I continued working most of the rest of the summer.

With only a few weeks remaining before the start of school, Jerry and I craved some vacation time. If we were to continue working, we figured our time was more valuable than our sixty–five cents an hour wage. So we asked for a raise. Our supervisor declined, so Jerry and I responded that since he wouldn't give us a raise we were quitting.

The supervisor said to be fair, we needed to give him a week or two's notice so that he could find replacements. "How much notice would you have given Jerry and me if you'd fired us?" I asked.

"Well, I don't know."

"That's just what I thought," I said.

If somebody had said to me, "You really think you're hot stuff, don't you?" it would have made me angry and I would have denied it. But it would have been right on target.

"I don't know how you will ever save enough for college with your lazy attitude," Mom said about my quitting. "And I don't know how you will succeed in college or at anything, if you don't learn to stick to things and to apply yourself."

One Saturday when we were walking to the grocery, Mom reached over to pick up a penny.

"What would you do to save a penny?" I asked her.

"I don't know. I try to save wherever I can," she said.

"Would you walk a mile just to save a penny?"

"Yes. We need every penny we can get just to make ends meet," she answered.

Somehow, I got the message. During the afternoons and on weekends while school was in session, and every summer, I worked at a number of jobs to save for college. Then I worked through-out college, as well.

Mom had three physical weaknesses: migraine headaches, for which she could do little but go to bed and cover her forehead with Analgesic Balm; high blood pressure, for which she took medicine; and weak ankles, for which she could do nothing.

Every three or four months, she would turn an ankle walking to or from work. Whenever it happened she would also fall down, sometimes further hurting herself and usually damaging or soiling her clothing.

When she sprained an ankle on the way home, she would limp home and soak her swollen ankle in a bucket of hot water and Epsom salts. But when it happened after leaving home, she would hobble to her job at the Kroger warehouse as best she could, work all day with a throbbing ankle and then limp home in the evening. Sometimes the pain made her ill.

Once, just before sitting down to eat with a bunch of church kids, the leader asked me to deliver the grace. At home we never prayed over our food; we just ate it. (I always ate as fast as I could so I would at least get my share.) I stood there, unable to say anything. Finally, a girl my age jumped in and gave the grace.

It was as though the covers had been yanked back, revealing my spiritual puniness for everyone to see. I felt more naked than when the Scouts took my pants off.

After that experience, I memorized several table graces so I would never have to go through that again.

But I still had trouble praying. Prayers from the Episcopal Book of Common Prayer seemed perfect to me. Whenever I tried to pray on my own, even in my own head, the ideas and words sounded pretty stupid.

I couldn't even pray right. Thinking up words anything like those in the Book of Common Prayer was beyond me. And I told myself that God had much better things to do than listening to all of my stupidity.

Little old lady, chuckling

Our church choir sang twice on Christmas Eve, first at five thirty and then for an eleven p.m. service lighted by hundreds of candles.

After the first service, we'd tour the hospitals at the Indiana University Medical Center, singing carols to patients. (We also did this every Easter morning).

Next, we would be treated to dinner at the Columbia Club, a rich Republicans' club next to the church on the Circle. Always the same thing was served—split–pea soup, chicken a la King, fruit salad, and hard dinner rolls. I liked everything. And having it just once a year didn't make me tired of it.

Jerry Caldwell said the Columbia Club treated us to dinner because the Columbia Club was built with one foot of their building sitting on Christ Church property. I wasn't sure he was right but didn't say so. Jerry was plenty smart and had a good story for everything. But I figured that the Columbia Club was just being neighborly.

After dinner, we also were guests of the Circle Theatre, where we got to see whatever was playing absolutely free. The theater was at least one hundred yards from the church, so Jerry didn't claim it was encroaching upon church property.

This was the Christmas I had just turned twelve.

We had looked at the movie for maybe ten minutes. Jerry and I agreed with Jim Scott that the movie wasn't worth watching. All that kissing and such!

We were eating popcorn in the balcony, which we had all to ourselves because of the boring movie and the fact that it was Christmas Eve.

Fewer than half the seats on the main floor were occupied. But after practicing on empty seats, we decided we could bomb twenty or thirty people with popcorn by moving along the edge of the balcony. Thirty drops, thirty hits. About the time our first targets stopped watching for us, we would return to them and run the cycle again.

We became skillful, lining up the puffy kernels at nose level, right between our eyes, and dropping them. We'd watch the white missiles fall, half like a rock and half like a feather, until they bounced off a bald head or caught in a tangle of hair.

Then we'd draw our heads back behind the balcony railing and laugh through our noses, all proud of ourselves. When an usher appeared and looked at us suspiciously, we smiled like choir boys, watched the show and ate at our popcorn. After the coast was clear, we resumed our popcorn attack from different seats.

The next time the usher showed up, it was to escort us from the theater.

"The management lets you guys in for free and then you act like a bunch of jerks," was all he had to say.

We went to the Sunday school area in the basement of the church and sat dejectedly with an hour and a half to kill before the next service. I volunteered that the movie hadn't been worth a hoot anyway. But that didn't make us feel much better.

Jim said it was unfair of the usher to kick us out. Jerry and I readily agreed. The more we talked the more certain we were that our case had not been fairly adjudicated. Heck, there had been no due process about it whatsoever! We had not even been accused of a crime, let alone given an opportunity to deny it.

Even though we had been the only occupants of the balcony and even though we each had a bag of popcorn, wasn't such evidence entirely circumstantial?

The guilty party could easily have been a little old lady who would sneak upstairs and drop popcorn on unsuspecting patrons below and then hustle back downstairs, just to make the usher think it was us. She could have been chuckling away about it, even as we discussed it.

I don't know if we saw the poster board before or after we came up with our idea, but there it was inviting our use. We each authored biting protest remarks. Mine declared boldly in the blackest of crayon:

Circle Theater
Unfair to Kids!

Then we picketed in circular protest under the theater marquee, appealing our plight to all who would pass our way.

But nobody passed our way. Other than shadowy heads in a few passing cars, we didn't see a soul. After a while, two unkempt men approached like they were choreographed to be tipsy. We were encouraged when one stepped boldly forward. But instead of offering support for our cause, he wanted to know whether we had any spare change.

Never one to underestimate the power of public relations, Jerry gave each a dime.

The lady selling tickets and the usher who tore them in two noticed us and huddled. Soon three ushers, the woman in white who'd sold us popcorn and an older man I figured to be the manager looked out at us. Then they started laughing. This certainly wasn't the reaction we'd counted upon. I thought the manager was going to fall down laughing.

Soon three ushers, the woman in white who'd
sold us popcorn and an older man I figured
to be the manager looked out at us.

For ten more freezing minutes we waved our placards at passing motorists, but they paid us little heed.

I don't know whether it was the cold or the lack of success that got to us first. Jerry just said, "Let's go." So we jammed the placards into a trash can, grabbed our ears to keep them from falling off and followed red noses back to church.

Cooties are almost a thing of the past. Thanks should go to Grandma's Pine Tar Soap, which we used to scrub our scalps. I never had cooties and I don't recall Fred complaining about them either.

Now with the passing of cooties, the cootie catcher also has nearly disappeared from the American scene. Nobody mourns the cootie. But I mourn the pending extinction of the cootie catcher.

Of course cootie catchers have a secondary use (other than chomping cooties). And it was this secondary use to which my friends and I put them—namely, cootie catcher fights.

From the start, it should be pointed out that a cootie catcher never attacks a human being.

Instead, when there are no cooties for cootie catchers to devour, a cootie catcher will viciously attack another cootie catcher. Sadly, cootie catcher fights always end with the annihilation of one of the two cootie catchers.

Church bulletins are an ideal size for making cootie catchers. Any self-respecting church bulletin is good for the construction of at least two cootie catchers. And sermons offer ample time for several cootie catcher fights.

With the dimming of the lights, when all congregational eyes are on the minister, and with all of the ladies' hand fans muffling the sound, boys in the choir may feel free to tear paper for the construction of cootie catchers. As soon as it is constructed, of course, the cootie catcher attacks any other cootie catcher in sight.

Wise cootie catchers know to avoid attacking from the front, instead flanking the enemy and ripping him at the back flaps of the finger holds.

Wait! Everyone needs a cootie catcher to understand this maneuver.

Cootie catchers are easy to construct. But it is important that they be made with care.

They are constructed in the following manner:

First, select top-quality paper. The better the paper, the finer the cootie catcher! Clay-coated stock is especially good. Regular paper, sized eight and a half inches by eleven, is too big for warfare. Narrower is better—no wider than seven inches or so.

Now for the construction (please also follow the diagram):

1. The first task is to make a square piece of paper. With paper in a position ready to be written upon, take the upper right–hand corner of the paper and move it to the far side so that the top edge of the paper lines up with the left edge. Make it exact and then use a thumbnail to crease the diagonal. All creases should be made with precision and as fine as a knife blade. The excess paper at the bottom should now be removed. Fold the paper at the edge line created below what had been the

right edge of the paper. (Of course, the right edge now parallels the bottom of the paper). After using a thumbnail to make a sharp edge, tear the excess paper off in order to end up with a square piece of paper.

2. Unfold the paper. Then fold and crease a second diagonal so that an X is formed across the paper. Both sharp creases should be on the same paper surface. Make certain the fold perfectly dissects the corners. Then unfold the paper again and place it with the creases of the X on top.

3. Now pick a corner and place the point in the exact middle of the two dissecting diagonals and crease the fold. Move around the paper doing the same thing with each point of the paper until something resembling a square envelope is made.

4. Turn the whole thing over so that a small square paper with no flaps is faceup. Now pick a corner and perfectly match it with the center just like before and crease the angled fold. Now move around the paper repeating the same process with each point of the paper.

Crease those folds like knife blades. Be exact so the corners don't fold over one another.

5. Press an index finger at the very center of the paper faceup. Pick it up and improve upon the folds both vertically and horizontally, which when folded over create rectangles twice as long as they are wide. The index finger should be removed to keep it from getting mashed in the process. Take the side which has four flaps of single-width paper and create pockets out of each section. Crease these outward-pointing folds one more time.

Ta–da! The cootie catcher is finished. There are pockets for thumb, index finger, middle finger and a fourth pocket for the two smaller fingers.

Notice that the cootie catcher has a double-hinged mouth. This always fools cooties and, strange as it may sound, other cootie catchers.

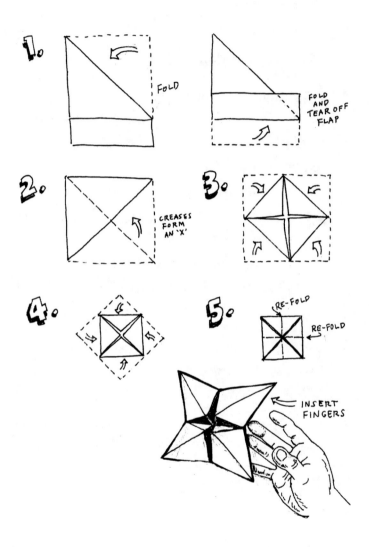

1. FOLD

FOLD AND TEAR OFF FLAP

2. CREASES FORM AN 'X'

3.

4.

5. RE-FOLD
RE-FOLD

INSERT FINGERS

One Sunday, Bobby Love sang a solo in place of a Sunday anthem:

"Oh, for the wings, for the wings of a dove!
Far away, far away would I roam.
In the wilderness build me a nest,
And remain there forever at rest.
Far away! Far away!
Far away, far away would I roam."

The ladies of the congregation liked Bobby's song so much he had to sing it two Sundays straight. Odd words for a church message nevertheless. A bird's idea of paradise, one has to suspect. "In my Father's house are many mansions."

While Bobby sang, the ladies of the congregation would get their Flanner & Buchanan Funeral Home fans fluttering. It sounded like a whole flock of doves flapping their wings. The church interior was painted in shades of green and deep purple, depicting grapevines, bunches of grapes and lots of leaves. And you could pick out plenty of good places for doves to build nests and remain, if not forever at rest, at least until the church was repainted.

When Bobby got done and the minister blessed the offering, the lights dimmed and it was time for the sermon. But those fans kept on fluttering, which was great because the sound muffled and blended right in with fighting cootie catchers.

They don't make much noise when they fight—those soft bodies of theirs coming together.

And when they tear apart in death they never scream nor cry out. Brave little creatures!

The most outstanding cootie catcher I ever constructed (very possibly ever constructed by anybody) survived the choir loft campaigns of three sermons—actually two and three fourths sermons.

This particular cootie catcher had the uncanny ability to attack enemy cootie catchers' finger flaps, ripping away before the newly-constructed enemy knew what hit it.

The abilities of this cootie catcher were of great concern to Jerry Caldwell and Jim Scott who witnessed the violent destruction of their finest cootie catchers.

After the second Sunday, this heroic cootie catcher should have been retired, bronzed and given its rightful place in *The Cootie Catcher Hall of Fame,* instead of being expected to engage in additional campaigns. Its teeth were badly blunted, for goodness sake!

Nevertheless, during the sermon that third Sunday, this valiant competitor ripped through both of Jerry's cootie catchers and one of Jim's.

But by then the bite had gone out of this great cootie catcher's teeth. Jim's second cootie catcher lashed back when the great one was no longer able to clamp tightly to a finger flap. And what was likely the most super-duper cootie catcher of all time was ripped to shreds.

Seeing its sad ending would have misted up anybody's eyes.

With a church program making two cootie catchers, this superstar outlasted eleven enemy cootie catchers (both of Jerry's and Jim's for two Sundays, both of Jerry's, and one of Jim's on that third Sunday).

None of us ever witnessed a cootie catcher that came close to matching this record. Jim had one that survived one and a half sermons. And he bragged on it.

Getting confirmed in the Episcopal Church sure wasn't easy. What made it even harder for me was that I had not attended Episcopal Sunday school. And I didn't pay much attention to Bible readings during church services.

Confirmation candidates had to successfully complete months of catechism classes. Father Powell believed that when it came to training up young minds on behalf of the Lord, there was no substitute for memory work. He assigned it by the tome.

To be honest, his assignments were difficult but doable. Until the last few weeks of classes,

I had managed to keep fully up to date with my memory work, which I dutifully recited to Father Powell. Then with just two weeks left, I got lax and came to class unprepared.

I was one of the youngest kids in the class. Ned was older and always seemed to know exactly what he was doing. I told him how worried I was about not being prepared.

"Look," he said. "Nobody memorizes this stuff. Just take your catechism book to Father Powell and tell him you already recited these passages, and he'll check 'em off. He does that for everybody. He never questions it."

"Honesty is the best policy," Mom always said. I knew she was right. I also knew that I was breaking one of the Ten Commandments—and to a minister! Nevertheless, I followed Ned's lead.

"Yes sir. This section and this one, too," I told the elderly pastor, who smiled and checked them off.

That week and the next, Father Powell continued to check off sections which I had not memorized but claimed to have recited.

And he did so for Ned and for a small fraternity of others as well.

On Sunday I would be confirmed and become eligible to receive Holy Communion, our Savior's body and blood.

I had thought a lot about telling lies to Father Powell and about God's commandment concerning false witness. I figured Father Powell wasn't far behind St. Paul on God's list of favorite people. If I was even on any of God's lists, I knew I must be near the bottom and still moving down.

I also thought about Pinocchio and my nose, which seemed to be sticking out more than most kids'.

But before long it was my turn to kneel in front of Bishop Kirchhoffer. Cupping his hands on my head, he prayed:

"Defend, oh Lord, this Thy child, Donald, with Thy heavenly grace that he may continue Thine forever; and daily increase in Thee, more and more, until he comes unto Thy everlasting kingdom. Amen."

In addition to my dishonesty with Father Powell, I had started to cuss. I was careful who was around and I didn't use the Lord's name in vain. But I thought the guys at school were really impressed with my hells and damns.

I loaned a quarter to Fred. After a couple of weeks, I asked him when he was going to pay me back. But he had forgotten and said he didn't owe me anything.

"You son of a *bleep*," I shouted at him.

"Do you know what you just said?" he asked.

"You just called our mother a terrible thing. You just called Mom a dog."

When I realized what a rotten thing I'd said, I started to cry in honest anguish. I wasn't a crier. I made it my business not to cry whenever I got hurt because crying was for cry-babies. I couldn't even remember when I'd last cried.

"I'm sorry. I didn't know it. I didn't mean to say anything bad about Mom," I pleaded.

"It's really stupid to call people things you don't even understand. When you call your brother a son of a dog, you're calling yourself one, too." I didn't care about that. I was just terribly sorry about saying something nasty about Mom.

Despite this jolt, my cussing continued. But I proceeded with care to avoid cussing around home or at church. Then one day Mom asked me to do something I thought was entirely unneces-sary, and out came a curse word!

Before I knew what hit me, Mom slapped me hard across the cheek. Instant justice was called for and delivered. Again, I found myself crying and apologizing. What a louse I had become.

But I didn't know how lucky I was. Mom's slap had stopped my cursing in its tracks!

Unfortunately, the problem of my smart-aleck mouth continued.

After choir practice on Friday nights, some of us guys would go to Haag's drugstore for a Coke or some ice cream. Haag's comic book rack was out of sight of the cash register. Though I never stole anything else, my buddies and I stole comic books on several occasions.

Once, when we were climbing down from soda fountain stools, the druggist ran over and grabbed a shabby-looking man who had tried to steal a bottle of whiskey by attempting to hide it under his ragged coat.

"Aren't you ashamed?" he asked the man. "What kind of an example do you think you're setting for these boys?"

The man had a red nose and sorrowful eyes. I've never seen anyone look more ashamed. It might have been my choir buddies and I who had set the bad example for him, instead of the other way around.

Somehow, I felt as ashamed of stealing comic books as the man appeared to feel. Maybe the other guys felt the same way. I doubt any of us stole comic books again.

"Donald" was a sissy name and "Donny" was babyish. "Don" was mostly okay. When teachers called me Donald, as they always did, I inwardly flinched at the sissy sound of it.

Mine wasn't the only such name. Most guys had names that were equally sissified—Ronald and Dennis and Steven and William and James and Thomas and Richard and dozens more. All were sissy names in their extended formality, I believed.

I liked manly American names like Mark and Curt and Jack and John and Hank (which I didn't know came from Henry, which would have been almost as bad as Donald).

By the sixth grade, I started asking teachers to please call me Don. All ignored this request, continuing to call me Donald.

There were worse curses in my family than my name, and I had escaped all of the really bad ones. All, that is but one.

I saw red hair for boys as one such curse. Red hair was nice for girls but not for guys, in my growing-up opinion. Jammy's husband, my grandfather, had been redheaded, and so were Mom and my two sisters. Luckily, Fred and I escaped.

Another family curse was the name "Volney," which like a bad gene would skip randomly from one generation to another and then attach itself to some innocent kid or his cousin.

One of my grandmother's brothers was a Volney as were several of his descendants. I escaped. But like a birthmark under clothing, Volney showed up as Fred's middle name. It is true that "Vol" made a good nickname if you lived in Tennessee, the Volunteer State. And that's where several of our Volney relatives lived.

The curse of Aunt Lolly's nose was the one which attached itself to me. By the time I was twelve or thirteen, there was no mistaking it.

Unlike Bob Hope's ski-jump nose, which would have been good for laughs, mine grew to become like one of those playground slides with the hump in the middle. It would have served to hold glasses, but my eyesight was perfect. Someone told me to be proud of my nose and to think of it as regal. Instead, I pitied kings everywhere who had such noses.

My choir buddy, Jerry, had a nose that was so small it failed even to keep his glasses in place. Jerry fought a constant and losing battle to keep his heavy glasses at the top of his nose. Jerry's glasses were pretty thick and he couldn't see much of anything without them.

I told him that if we could figure out how to do it, I'd take half of his glasses if he would take some of my nose.

Fred, age 13, Don, 8

Basso profundo

Pop Raymond was a big man any way you measured him.

He also was the best singer in our choir. Pop farmed some land near Rushville and drove to Indianapolis for choir practice Friday night and for Sunday church.

Whoever thought up "basso profundo" had Pop Raymond in mind, with his profoundly deep bass voice. I figured he could have been an opera star if he hadn't liked farming so much. I remember him singing the bass solo from Handel's *Messiah* where the words from the King James Bible are:

Thus saith the Lord, the Lord of hosts. And yet in a little while and I will shake; and I will shake; (each "shake" drawn out over two dozen notes) all nations, I'll shake; the Heavens, the earth, the seas, the dry land— all nations, I'll shake.

Haggai 2:6

Well, Pop put his whole self into it. And did he shake! I couldn't help but watch his belly.

Pop must have been over sixty when his wife contracted tuberculosis and was moved into a sanitarium. Pop needed to reorient his life in order to remain close to her. That included resigning from the choir.

We had a celebration in his honor. And he was told how much the choir would miss him.

"I don't think you'll miss me for long," was all he said. I believe he really thought that was true. But he was wrong. There was never another Pop Raymond. Nobody else in the choir ever sang as well. And I'd guess no one had his deep, heavyset character.

The choir loved singing *The Messiah,* George Frederick Handel's great masterwork. The choirmaster said many of the passages are from the Old Testament, foretelling the coming of Jesus, as well as passages from the New Testament reflecting the fulfillment of the Messianic prophecy. Handel appointed a noted theologian to select verses for the music. The King James Bible passages (slightly altered in places to fit the music) are quoted in the order of appearance in *The Messiah* by Handel:

> Comfort ye, comfort ye my people, saith your God. Speak ye comfortably to Jerusalem, and cry unto her, that her warfare is accomplished, that her iniquity is pardoned. ... The voice of him that crieth in the wilderness, prepare ye the way of the Lord, make straight in the desert a highway for our God. Every valley shall be exalted, and every mountain and hill ... made low ... the crooked straight, and the rough places plain. And the glory of the Lord shall be revealed, and all flesh shall see it together: for the mouth of the Lord hath spoken it.
>
> Isaiah 40: 1–5

Thus saith the Lord of hosts; yet once ... a little while, and I will shake the Heavens, and the earth, the sea and the dry land. ... And the desire of all nations shall come ... .

Haggai 2: 6–7

The Lord, whom ye seek, shall suddenly come to His temple, even the messenger of the covenant, whom ye delight in: behold, He shall come, saith the Lord of hosts. But who may abide the day of His coming? And who shall stand when He appeareth? For He is like a refiner's fire ... and He shall purify the sons of Levi, ... that they may offer unto the Lord an offering in righteousness.

Malachi 3: 1–3

Behold a virgin shall conceive, and bear a son, and shall call His name Emmanuel, "God–with–us."

Isaiah 7: 14

O thou that tellest good tidings to Zion, get thee up into the high mountain; O thou that tellest good tidings to Jerusalem, lift up thy voice with strength; lift it up, be not afraid; say unto the cities of Judah, Behold your God!

Isaiah 40: 9

Arise, shine; for thy light is come, and the glory of the Lord is risen upon thee. For, behold…darkness shall cover the earth, and gross darkness the people; but the Lord shall rise upon thee, and His glory shall be seen upon thee. And the Gentiles shall come to thy light and kings to the brightness of thy rising.

Isaiah 60: 1–3

The people that walked in darkness have seen a great light; and they that dwell in the land of the shadow of death, upon them hath the light shined.

Isaiah 9: 2

For unto us a child is born, unto us a Son is given; and the government shall be upon His shoulder; and His name shall be called Wonderful, Counselor, The Mighty God, The Everlasting Father, The Prince of Peace.

Isaiah 9: 6

There were shepherds abiding in the field, keeping watch over their flocks by night. And lo, the angel of the Lord came upon them, and the glory of the Lord shone round about them; and they were sore afraid. And the angel said unto them, Fear not: for behold, I bring you good tidings of great joy, which shall be to all people. For unto you is born this day in the city of David a Savior, which is Christ the Lord. And suddenly there was with the angel a multitude of the heavenly host praising God, and saying.... Glory to God in the highest, and peace on earth, good will toward men.

Luke 2:8–11,13–14

Rejoice greatly, O daughter of Zion; shout, O daughter of Jerusalem; behold, thy King cometh unto thee; He is the righteous Savior...and He shall speak peace unto the heathen.

Zechariah 9: 9–10

Then shall the eyes of the blind be opened, and the ears of the deaf...unstopped. Then shall the lame man leap as an hart, and the tongue of the dumb shall sing....

Isaiah 35:5–6

He shall feed His flock like a shepherd; and He shall gather the lambs with His arm, and carry them in His bosom, and...gently lead those that are with young.

Isaiah 40:11

Come unto Him, all ye that labor and are heavy laden, and He will give you rest. Take His yoke upon you, and learn of Him, for He is meek and lowly of heart; and ye shall find rest unto your souls. ... His yoke is easy, and His burden is light.

Matthew 11:28–20–30

Behold, the Lamb of God, that taketh away the sins of the world!

John 1:29

He was despised and rejected of men; a man of sorrow, and acquainted with grief....

Isaiah 53:3

He gave His back to the smiters, and His cheeks to them that plucked off the hair. He did not hide His face from shame and spitting.

Isaiah 50:6

Surely He hath borne our griefs, and carried our sorrows. ... He was wounded for our transgressions, He was bruised for our iniquities; the chastisement of our peace was upon Him.... And with His stripes we are healed. All we like sheep have gone astray; we have turned every one to his own way;

and the Lord hath laid on Him the iniquity of us all.

Isaiah 53:4–6

All they that see Him laugh Him to scorn; they shoot out their lips, and shake their heads, saying, He trusted in God that He would deliver Him; let Him deliver Him, if He delight in Him.

Psalm 22:7–8

Thy rebuke hath broken His heart; He is full of heaviness; He looked for some to have pity on Him, but there was no man; neither found He any to comfort Him.

Psalm 69:20

Behold, and see if there be any sorrow like unto His sorrow....

Lamentations 1:12

He was cut off out of the land of the living; for the transgressions of Thy people was He stricken.

Isaiah 53:8

But Thou didst not leave His soul in Hell; nor didst Thou suffer Thy Holy One to see corruption.

Psalm 16:10

Lift up your heads, O ye gates; and be ye lift up, ye everlasting doors; and the King of Glory shall come in. Who is this King of Glory? The Lord strong and mighty, the Lord mighty in battle. Lift up your heads, O ye gates; and be ye lift up, ye everlasting doors; and the King of Glory shall come in. Who is this King of Glory? The Lord of hosts, He is the King of Glory.

Psalm 24:7–10

Unto which of the angels said He at any time, thou art my son, this day have I begotten thee?...Let all the angels of God worship Him.

Hebrews 1:5–6

Thou art gone up on high, Thou hast led captivity captive; and received gifts for men; yea, even for Thine enemies, that the Lord God might dwell among them.

Psalm 68:18

The Lord gave the word: great was the company of the preachers.

Psalm 68:11

How beautiful are the feet of them that preach the gospel of peace, and bring glad tiding of good things!... Their sound is gone

out unto all lands and their words unto the
ends of the world.

Romans 10:15

Why do the nations so furiously rage
together...why do the people imagine a
vain thing? The kings of the earth rise up,
and the rulers take counsel together, against
the Lord, and against His anointed.... Let us
break their bonds asunder, and cast away
their yokes from us. He that dwelleth in
Heaven shall laugh them to scorn; the Lord
shall have them in derisions. Thou shalt
break them with a rod of iron; Thou shalt
dash them in pieces like a potter's vessel.

Psalm 11:1–4, 9

(And the "Hallelujah Chorus" which Jammy
loved): Hallelujah, for the Lord God omnip-
otent reigneth.

Revelation 19:6

I know that my Redeemer liveth, and that
He shall stand at the latter day upon the
earth; and though...worms destroy this
body, yet in the flesh shall I see God.

Job 19:25–26

For now is Christ risen from the dead...the
first fruits of them that sleep.... Since by

man came death, by man came also the resurrection of the dead. For as in Adam all die, even so in Christ shall be made alive.

1 Corinthians 15:20–22

Behold, I tell you a mystery. We shall not all sleep, but we shall all be changed. In a moment, in the twinkling of an eye at the last trumpet.... The trumpet shall sound, and the dead shall be raised incorruptible, and we shall be changed. For this, corruptible must put on incorruption, and this mortal must put on immortality.... Then shall be brought to pass the saying that is written, Death is swallowed up in victory. The sting of death is sin; and the strength of sin is the law. But thanks be to God, who giveth us the victory through our Lord Jesus Christ.

1 Corinthians 15:51–57

If God be for us who can be against us? Who shall lay anything to the charge of God's elect? God that justifieth. Who is he that condemneth? It is Christ that died, yea rather, that is risen again, who is ... at the right hand of God, who ... makes intercession for us.

Romans 8:31, 33–34

Worthy is the Lamb that was slain. ... And
hath redeemed us to God by His blood. ... To
receive power, and riches, and wisdom, and
strength, and honor, and glory and blessing. ... Blessing and honor and glory and
power, be unto Him that sitteth upon the
throne, and unto the Lamb for ever and
ever. ... Amen

Revelation 5:12, 9, 12–14

A sink with a marble top sat in a hall near the
choir room behind the church nave. I expect
it had been there since the dawn of plumbing.
Over it and to the right was a hook, and on the
hook was a copper cup. The cup was dented and
tinged green with age. Water is colder and tastes
better when it goes into your mouth by way of a
copper cup.

Everybody I ever knew who was thirsty when
they passed the sink got themselves a drink
of water using that copper cup. I used it. Jerry
Caldwell used it. Father Powell used it, and so did
Bishop Kirchhoffer.

Even the fine ladies of St. Agnes Guild who tended the altar took water from this same cup, though they first rinsed off the lip, I noticed.

The choir boys had a warm-up routine that involved going up and down the scale—a lot like a basketball team shooting layups before a game. The words we used on the way up the scale were repeated on the way down:

"Copper kettles carry comfort, killing cough and cold. Tinkers take their turn at tea until their tale is told."

While singing that warm-up drill, I thought of the copper cup (never mind that it wasn't a kettle) as carrying comfort, killing cough and cold.

More likely it was closer to copper cups are killing comfort, carrying cough and cold, instead of the other way around. Since nobody I knew died during the time they drank water from the cup, maybe we didn't need to worry about what we didn't know.

Another vocal drill tested me and I flunked. As a matter of fact, only a few passed. It had to do with starting at middle C. Middle C was "one." We were tested separately, like singing a solo. In turn we sang up the octave scale, returning to middle C after each step up the scale:

"One–two, one–three, one–four, one–five, one–six, one–seven, one–eight, one."

The hard intervals for me were one-six and one–seven. "My Bonnie lies over the ocean" starts out with one–six—"My Bon." So I got to where I could get one-six. But I never could get one-seven. Somebody told me that "Ba–li," of "Bali Hi will call you" from a song in *South Pacific* was a one–seven interval. But still it eluded me.

Executioners

During the early part of the Twentieth Century, a fine system of single-car electric trains had served Indiana. Called interurbans, the cars drew electricity from overhead feeder lines and carried passengers between larger towns and cities until the private automobile put them out of business.

Indianapolis streetcars, and some of the tracks they ran on, were vestiges of the interurban system.

I frequently rode streetcars on Washington and Michigan streets. Later these became trolley lines. In Indianapolis trolleys rode on rubber tires, instead of steel wheels and tracks, and derived electric power from twin overhead feeds, instead of a single feed. Indianapolis trolleys never "clanged" though the streetcars did. So you couldn't sing, "Clang, clang, clang went the trolley," like Judy Garland sang in *Meet Me in St. Louis.* In Indianapolis to be accurate, you'd have to sing, "Clang, clang, clang went the streetcar." Finally, buses were assigned to all the routes, and streetcars and trolleys were history.

My favorite ride was on the streetcar to Broad Ripple. Fred and I rode the Broad Ripple streetcar to visit Chuck Morris, a church friend nearly my brother's age. Whenever we got to the place where the houses ended, the conductor shoved the throttle forward, and the streetcar would reach speeds we guessed to be more than sixty miles per hour.

Chuck said that if the conductor pushed all the way forward on the throttle and if the track were long enough and straight enough, the streetcar would continue to accelerate indefinitely. We supposed he was right.

Chuck lived in an apartment in downtown Broad Ripple. All sorts of neat things were within easy walking distance. Broad Ripple Park had the biggest swimming pool around. And if you had the money, you could rent a canoe or a pedal boat at the park to explore the White River.

We liked to walk on the railroad trestle over the White River and explore the wild, wooded area across the river.

Chuck taught us to first listen for a train and then place a hand on the track to feel for vibrations. The final test was to place your ear to the track and listen for vibrations. If each test proved negative, it was safe to start across.

To be fully safe, Chuck performed the tests one third of the way and again two thirds of the way across. Then if we detected a train, we would have time to hurry off the trestle.

We felt the vibration of trains a few times before starting across the trestle and simply waited for the trains to pass. Every fifteen feet or so, a particularly long crosstie extended beyond the edge of the trestle to help support the overhead structure.

If somehow we ever got stranded in the middle of the trestle in the face of an on–rushing train, Chuck instructed us to climb out on one of these long ties. We'd be safe from the train out there, though it would be pretty scary, he said.

Once, Chuck also took us to a butcher shop to watch them chop off chicken heads. Blood flew with each whack of the cleaver. And the area was full of dead chickens, most quivering and some flopping. Flopping ones continued to splatter blood. White feathers filled the air. I know, because one got in my gaping mouth!

That day six or eight kids showed up to watch, and the two executioners seemed to enjoy being the center of so much attention. To get a better look, Fred crowded forward and got too close to a quivering chicken. An unexpected final disjointed leap sent a swirl of blood onto his trousers.

Feeling guilty
about doing good

Nearly every kid loved going to Riverside Amusement Park. This was an expensive outing. I remember going only twice. You paid to get through the front gate. And to top it off, each ride cost extra! But what kept us from going back for more visits wasn't the cost.

Our second visit was on the Fourth of July. All the rides had lines. We had ridden the merry-go-round, the roller coaster, the dodge-'ems (electric cars that you banged into other people's cars and tried to avoid getting bumped in return) and the shoot-the-chute (a boat ride through a darkened tunnel that finally led up an incline for a concluding, headfirst splashy plunge into the loading pool).

Fred and I also worked our way through the house of mirrors. I remember a couple of mirrors, one of which made me look hideously fat and the other even skinnier than I was.

People say "hot as the Fourth of July," and it was days like this one they had in mind. Mom packed a baloney sandwich and an apple for each of us, which she carried in a paper sack.

Just before noon Mom said we should eat. She was concerned about the lunchmeat spoiling in the heat. We bought some Cokes and despite the crowd found an empty bench, thinking we were lucky to find it.

We were chewing up the first bites of our sandwich. High overhead a guy on the Ferris wheel lost a battle between vertigo and a greasy breakfast and heaved sour bile down upon our heads. Sitting in the center, I was the primary target, Mom and Fred secondary and peripheral.

The Ferris wheel was full and had stopped for occupants to commence the dismounting process. There was a sprinkling of applause—for the man's marksmanship, one supposes. Others laughed, but the humor eluded us.

Mom came up with a few paper napkins which she repeatedly washed in a drinking fountain to wipe our faces. Despite the effort the stench was overpowering, and I was still picking lumps from my ears.

The bus ride downtown was packed. We found ourselves standing at the back of the bus. The people we were standing over quickly gave up their seats to us and tried to push their way to the front of the bus. But the driver was letting as many of the holiday crowd onto the bus as it would hold, thwarting their best efforts.

Every unopened window on the bus was soon open. Nearby, everyone held handkerchiefs or sleeves to their noses and leaned as far away from us as they could manage.

After arriving downtown, we decided to walk the final mile home instead of using our transfers. Sometimes, misery hates company.

That was one week we didn't have to wait until Saturday night for a bath!

Every summer I looked forward to the Kroger Employee Family Picnic.

There was everything imaginable to eat—fried chicken, ham, baked beans, potato salad and sliced tomatoes as well as cake, pie and ice cream for dessert.

Then we would play free bingo until every family had won at least one bag of groceries.

There were games both for kids and adults. Some games were just for fun—like hopping races in burlap bags or passing potatoes chin–to–chin in team relays. Others were for prizes, such as the competition I had been looking forward to for weeks, "the twelve-and-under baseball toss."

I was nearly thirteen and knew it was my last chance to win. I also figured it was my turn, since boys older than I had always won in previous years.

As always before, the prize for throwing a baseball and hitting the target was a new mitt. My own mitt was a really cheap job. This one was of high quality.

But you may not understand what ended up being my problem, unless you have experienced sitting on a bus only to have all the seats fill up and have a woman get on and stand right over you. Of course, you would then feel compelled to stand up and give her your seat, even though you'd much rather sit than stand.

My only competition for the mitt was a six-year-old boy. The man in charge of setting up the baseball–toss competition made the target so close that even a six–year–old could hardly miss. When the little boy was given the first turn and threw and missed, I knew I had a problem. That was because everyone sighed with regret.

So I intentionally missed, thinking the kid would hit the target on his next toss. But he didn't. After a few more times, it became an embarrassment continuing to miss such an easy target. And I was growing tired of what came close to cheers when I did miss.

So I hit the target, won the glove to everyone's disappointment, and when nobody was looking, handed it to the kid and walked away. I thought that was that, but it wasn't.

Soon the kid's dad came up to me and told me what "a fine young man" I was and how he hoped his son would grow up to be just like me.

I didn't tell him how badly I wanted the mitt, that I didn't want to give it to his son and that I couldn't understand why a six–year–old kid needed a mitt, anyway. And I didn't tell him about how I'd lied to Father Powell and cussed, swiped comic books nor any of the rest.

And I certainly didn't tell him he would not want his son to grow up and be like me.

Instead, I just stood there in my embarrassment and tried to arrange a look on my face which said that, in all humility, I truly was "a fine young man." What I felt like was that I couldn't win for losing. I couldn't even pull off a good deed without feeling guilty.

Aunt Les and Uncle Blain lived on a farm near Greenfield, the New Castle bus' second stop east of Indianapolis. Uncle Blain was Mom's cousin.

At least once a summer, we would catch the Greyhound bus and ride as far as Greenfield, where Uncle Blain would pick us up in his 1934 Ford.

Fred and I got to ride in the rumble seat. It was fun bouncing along country roads and feeling the wind in my hair.

We had to cross three bridges, and whenever we headed across the longest of the three, the bridge over the Blue River, I'd say a silent prayer. The bridge had parallel boards for tires to aim at, and not only did it shake and rattle, I could actually see the steel superstructure moving overhead as the car passed underneath. But this just added to the thrill of the ride.

This particular trip to the farm was the same summer I gave up the mitt.

Boots, their shepherd dog, greeted us with sloppy licks. Then Fred and I headed out to the pasture to explore.

A creek Fred and I used to "swim" in ran through the pasture. More accurately, we had waded in ankle-deep muddy water. But it had seemed like the thing to do. The Hoosier poet, James Whitcomb Riley, had lived in Greenfield and written "The Ol' Swimmin' Hole," possibly about an enchanting spot along this same creek. Quite a ways downstream, one would have to conclude.

That summer, Uncle Blain's sow had recently birthed a litter of pigs and I tried unsuccessfully to catch one. I couldn't come close to catching any. Small pigs should not be underrated when it comes to speed, athleticism and agility.

Later, I saw the mother pig sleeping with her back shoved up against a fence that penned her away from her babies. Her fat back slopped through the fence, so I kicked at it, not hard enough to hurt her, just to see what she'd do.

She just grunted. The harder I kicked, the louder she'd grunt. Finally she lifted her head and looked hatefully back at me but refused to move.

After lunch, I headed for the pasture to see if I could get closer to catching one of the little pigs.

I started chasing the closest one, and he headed toward the rest of the litter which, I was startled to see, was grouped around the big sow. Apparently, Uncle Blain had let her into the pasture to feed her babies.

The sow took one look at me, accurately concluded I was trying to catch her baby, and started toward me with a shrieking snort. If you remember how steam locomotives pick up speed, then you know how fat sows run.

I took off as fast as I could in the opposite direction and got a nice head start. I didn't look back, but listening to her snorts, I could tell the sow was gaining on me. If she caught me, I knew I was history. I could hear her hard breathing just behind me as the fence grew taller in front of me.

That I was able to clear a fence nearly as tall as myself in a single bound would have seemed impossible. But I did it. When a kid is chased by an angry sow, his speed, athleticism and agility should not be underrated.

For dinner, Aunt Les would always kill two chickens.

Aunt Les' chickens weren't anything like store-bought chickens. First of all, they were hens—very well–fed hens. And because of their size, they bore a closer resemblance to turkeys than chickens. Aunt Les daily fed the hens, so they clustered about her trustfully whenever she went outside.

It was a simple matter for Aunt Les to scatter some feed on the ground, reach down and grab one of these stout hens by the head, and in one deft movement lift it and wring its neck before fear had a chance to pump any toughening fluid into the meat. The other hens continued to eat, so she could grab the second just as easily.

As soon as Aunt Les had plucked, cleaned, and sectioned these chickens, she coated them with egg and a mixture of flour and spices. Then without delay, she put them into a hot buttery skillet.

Aunt Les fried the chicken until each plump piece had a golden crust. When I bit into the thick white meat around the wishbone, it was impossible to keep all the juices in my mouth.

Turning down
a fortune

Jim Hunt's dad put a basketball goal up in the alley behind their house.

Jim and I played a lot of baseball, mostly just passing the ball or playing flies-and-grounders at Highland Park. In this game, the batter tossed the ball up and hit it to guys in the field. The first fielder to catch three balls—a combination of either flies or grounders—got to bat. We'd also choose up sides with other guys at the park and play seven innings of baseball most summer days.

But once I tried basketball, it became my real love.

I got to the point that I played basketball at every opportunity. I'd grab my well–worn ball as soon as school was out, as long as there was no snow on the alley. Rain–wet concrete didn't bother us, nor did the cold unless it was under twenty degrees.

There were six or eight regulars and at least as many not-so regulars who showed up to play. Sometimes we'd play three-on-three, but the alley was crowded with six players. So mostly we'd play two-on-two, usually with some other guys waiting to play the winners.

We also played H–O–R–S–E. This game is played with two or more players. Playing in turns, when the first player hits a shot of his choice, each suc-ceeding player must hit the same shot. Whoever misses such a shot gets an H, then an O, and so on until "horse" is spelled out, at which point that player is eliminated. The player left when everybody else is eliminated is the winner. For a shorter game, we'd play P–I–G.

I did not excel at these games because no one guarded me. Oddly, the closer someone guarded me the better I could hit, as long as they didn't foul me too severely.

Harold Carter came up with a golden basketball player which had been broken across the ankles. He worked at a company that made and sold trophies. The golden player had accidentally been broken from a trophy. He suggested that we hold a one-on-one tournament and give the golden basketball player to the winner. Harold did well in the tourney but was defeated by Nick.

I won my way to the final game where I also faced Nick, a big good-natured kid whose parents ran a Greek restaurant.

Rules were as follows: We scored just one point for each basket. We alternated possession after each made basket. We played to twenty–one, like in ping–pong. And like in ping–pong, we had to win by two points. Short of knocking an opponent down, there was no such thing as a foul. Alley–ball fouling must have been why the jump shot was developed—because when you jump, the ball and your hands doing the shooting are usually above the foul.

Nick took full advantage of his wide body and strength, moving into me when I shot, which was expected in alley ball. But Nick was better at it than any of the rest of us. With the score well into the thirties, I won on what Nick called another of my "impossibly lucky shots."

Later, Nick played varsity high school basketball at Tech High School. I couldn't even make the freshman team.

But it wasn't for lack of trying. More than four hundred freshmen boys went out for the team. At that time, Tech was the largest high school in the country and had been for the previous twenty years. But enrollment was down from more than ten thousand to less than seven thousand. It had been bigger before Howe High School opened farther out on the East Side. Tech had a large drop-out rate. If 2,500 freshmen started, only about half would graduate.

Most of the four hundred boys must have come out because their dads told them to—they sure couldn't play a lick. After a few days, only fifty remained. And in a couple of weeks it was down to the final cut. I was one of the last five guys to go.

The coach told us we would likely have made most other freshman teams. But the guys who made the Tech team were selected because they were better athletes than we were, not necessarily because they were better basketball players.

After the coach's talk, I didn't feel so badly. All of the guys who made the team were probably stronger or taller than I was. Of course, being tall is important in basketball. And frankly, I had little idea how to play organized basketball, using a full court, facing the basket. I was just an alley-ball player.

At that time the jump shot was a new invention, and Tech's freshmen players were not allowed to shoot jump shots. Instead, they were expected to play "fundamental basketball" which included the two–handed set shot and the one–handed push shot. In fact, the freshmen coach, Powell Morehead, was a member of the United States Olympic Basketball Committee, and he thought that players needed a foundation of fundamentals in order to excel.

But in a few years the jump shot took over as *the* fundamental shot. And for many years now, two–handed set shots and one–handed push shots have not been used. Better players at that time could hit these shots with deadly accuracy, until defensive–minded teams came along and demonstrated that by working aggressively such shots usually could be blocked. Jump shots, of course, were much harder to defend against.

Mr. Morehead invited me and another boy who also had been cut to work as student managers. We helped at practice and acted as referees during scrimmages. Playing strong teams from Indianapolis and Indiana's North Central Conference, this group of boys was undefeated both as freshmen and as sophomores on Tech's reserve team.

As a student manager, I got free tickets to varsity basketball games and sat free in some of the best reserved seats during the Indiana State High School Basketball Tournament. In those days, Indiana had a single tournament for high schools of all sizes.

Tech had one of its best varsity basketball teams ever my freshman year. I was late to the final Indianapolis Sectional game because of slow bus traffic. Crispus Attucks, an all–black high school and a big favorite to win the sectional, was ahead by ten or twelve points by the time I arrived halfway through the first half. Against all odds, Tech went on to win that game. Ultimately, Tech made it all the way to the final game of the state tournament only to lose badly to Muncie Central.

Outside Butler Fieldhouse, the evening of my way into that final game with Muncie, a man offered me fifty dollars for my ticket, which was four rows up, center court. Part of the 1986 movie *Hoosiers* was to be filmed in this fine old basketball hall. By the time the movie was made, it had been renamed Hinkle Fieldhouse in honor of Butler University's longtime multi–sport coach, Tony Hinkle.

I turned down the fifty bucks, which was a small fortune in 1952. The offer and my turn-down demonstrate how very important Indiana high school basketball was during that period.

The film classic *Hoosiers* was based upon a tiny high school from Milan, Indiana (called Hickory in the movie) winning the state tourney. It was said that it took every junior and senior boy to come up with enough boys for the Milan team. Whether or not that was true, this small high school really did win the Indiana State High School Basketball Tournament a few years after Tech lost it.

In the championship game of that tourney, Milan defeated Muncie Central High School, the same school that had whipped Tech so badly a few years earlier. The team was made up of a few good shooters, including Bobby Plump who hit the game–winning shot (just like in *Hoosiers*) with time running out against Muncie Central. Hard–working support players filled out the team. In Indiana, Milan is not pronounced like the city in Italy. Instead, it's pronounced like you'd say "my land" but without the "d" and with the accent on "My."

Along the way to the State Finals, Milan also defeated Crispus Attucks. Oscar Robertson, usually considered one of the best players to ever play the game, starred for that team. Attucks was State Champion the following year, and Oscar Robertson was named Indiana's "Mr. Basketball."

The area that ended up as Tech High School had started during the Civil War as an arsenal and military base. It didn't become a high school until 1912. The campus measured one half mile on each side and had a wrought iron fence boxing it in.

The school's full name was Arsenal Technical Schools—plural, to convey the fact that boys and girls could pursue a variety of trades, such as printing, home economics, airplane mechanics, office and clerical skills, commercial art, radio broadcasting, radio engineering, drafting and a variety of construction work skills. Or a student could opt for an academic curriculum, which is what I did.

Tech's enrollment was small when it first started. Mom had been in the first graduating class to attend all four years at Tech. And Jam had cooked and made her famous pies in the first cafeteria, which had started in the little brick guard house at the front gate across from where Arsenal Street runs into Michigan Street.

Jam baked the best pies I ever tasted. Anybody who ever tried them made the same claim.

Holding on for dear life

About the time I was honing my basketball skills, I also took up tennis. It wasn't long before I was hooked on the game.

I read an instructional book by tennis great Jack Kramer. And I worked hard to harness the power for my backhand that Kramer promised was there if I simply got my body into the proper alignment with the ball.

The forehand shot came pretty naturally. And the basic overhead smash and power serve seemed to be natural things to do, almost like throwing a baseball.

I had gotten polio when I was in junior high, but nobody knew it. It was thought to be the flu, as nearly as we could recall. I had noticed that muscles on one side of the small of my back were larger than those on the other side but I didn't think much about it. I figured it was from reaching over in baseball to catch grounders. In reality, muscles on the opposite side were stunted by the polio.

The polio left me with a slightly S-shaped spine, which I didn't know about at that time. I seemed to be able to do everything just like always and didn't pay any attention to the way my back looked. I learned about the polio when I went to the doctor for a permission slip to play on the high school tennis team. I had made "first man." This impressed my family, but that's because they hadn't seen the rest of our pathetic team.

But it wasn't the remains of polio that concerned the doctor. He instructed me to make an appointment with a heart specialist.

The heart specialist listened to my heart and ran some tests. Then his partner also listened to me. Finally, I was told I must never do anything strenuous as long as I lived. I was not even supposed to run to catch a bus.

"Are you trying to tell me that I can't play on the tennis team?" I wanted to know.

"You're never to play tennis again," the doctor answered.

"But high school tennis is no big deal. We hit the ball back and forth two or three times and then somebody messes up. So there isn't much running to it. Nobody gets out of breath or anything," I explained.

"You don't understand. You have a severe heart condition which will likely shorten your life."

"What are you saying? How long am I going to live?"

"Nobody can tell you that for certain. But if you follow my instructions and take it easy, I mean really take it easy, you might live to be thirty or so."

For the rest of the school year and throughout the summer, I followed the doctor's orders. I found a sedentary summer job and stayed away from athletic games and heavy work.

I also did a lot of thinking and plenty of feeling sorry for myself.

When the doctor had told me I might live to be as old as thirty, I guessed he was sugar–coating my prognosis. I thought I'd be lucky if I lived to be twenty–five.

I didn't tell anybody about my heart problem or my life expectancy. I would have felt funny doing so. And I figured people would think I was looking for sympathy. I supposed my family would talk to people and word would get around. But if any of my friends knew that their dogs might outlive me, none let on like they did. I asked God to help me. But I figured He remembered all the bad stuff I'd done. So why would He want to help me?

Then I looked up Dick Leary.

I wanted to talk to Dick for several reasons. I had known him all my life. And I thought he also had a weak heart, because I remembered he had contracted rheumatic fever as a little kid. So I thought he would understand my feelings. He was a good guy to talk to. It was like he knew lots of things, but first you had to ask him.

Dick poured each of us a cup of coffee. And we sat down at the kitchen table, drinking that rich adult brew like we always had. Dick drank his black. I still put milk and a little sugar in mine. He even struck and blew out a few wooden matches, let them cool and then bit off the ends.

"Dick, you ought to package those things and sell them for rat poison. They'd kill 'em dead. And you'd get rich!" I told him.

He grinned. "I see you're still the same old wiseacre," he responded.

"Yeah, but what I really think is those rats would be too smart to eat those things," I said to salvage all I could from the exchange.

We talked about our bad habits and said we ought to get rid of them once and for all. But we decided it's hard to break away from a bad habit.

"I don't think people can change as much as they want to or as much as other people want them to change—at least not without an all-out effort," Dick said. "Sometimes it takes a lifetime to do it."

Then I told him why I had come—what the doctor had told me. And I asked, "What do doctors tell you about your heart—because of the rheumatic fever that you had? How long do they think you will live, and so forth?"

"Oh, they listen to it. But they don't say much. They don't tell me it sounds bad, but they don't tell me it sounds good, either."

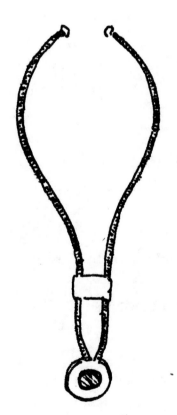

"Don't they at least tell you whether they think you will live a long time or not?" I persisted.

"They never have," he said. "Heck, I don't even think about it. None of us really knows how long we'll live. Maybe I'll die tomorrow. But chances are good I'm going to be around for a long time. I guess that's not much different from everybody else.

"We all have hearts that beat. And when

they stop, we die. I'm sure not going to waste time worrying about it.

"Even if I fall over dead in five minutes, I'm pretty lucky. My life's been good and my family's great. And I know I'll go to Heaven when I die."

That was really it wasn't it? I was scared about dying and not getting into Heaven because of all the bad stuff I'd done.

"You're pretty convinced about it, aren't you—about going to Heaven? How can you know you're going to Heaven?" I asked, because I'd never heard anybody claim they were certain of going to Heaven.

"Sure. I'm already enjoying eternal life. You don't have to die for that. It started when I was baptized and first believed in Jesus, so long ago I don't even remember when."

"I believe in Jesus," I told him. "It's just that I'm not such a good person."

"I'm no better than you," Dick said. "But that doesn't have anything to do with it, because we can't save ourselves.

"We can't even help. Jesus did it one–hundred percent. He lived to die for us and to remove all our sins—really to remove them for all time, so when we die we'll go to Heaven and be with Him.

"Jesus himself said so. And the Bible is filled with this great news. Jesus died even to save guys like you and me. Knowing that, we don't have to worry. Thanks to Jesus, dying is like going to sleep knowing you'll wake up in the morning.

"You remember that time Bob Gordon, Ben, and I pulled you from the river? Our Heavenly Father reaches His hand down to each of us like that through Jesus. I don't understand why everybody doesn't grab hold, just like you grabbed Bob."

Even if I fall over dead in five minutes,
I think I'm pretty lucky. ... My family's great.
And I know I'll go to Heaven when I die.

That fall I visited the heart specialist again. He looked at my records and then listened to my heart. His eyes grew wide. And I figured I was a dead duck for sure.

Then he called in his partner and he gave a listen. They looked at my record again, at each other, and finally they looked at me.

"This is close to a miracle," the first doctor said.

"This record says you have a heart that will cut your life short in only a few years. But now it sounds normal. You have a slight heart murmur, but I can hardly hear it. There's no reason why you can't lead a long and full life."

Getting pulled from the river flashed through my mind. But this time, God got the credit as well as the thanks.

Mr. Roobush offered to sell us his old Model–A Ford. And even though Mom didn't know how to drive, she bought it. Fred could drive and I was old enough for a beginner's permit.

The car was twenty–four years old. But it was in good shape and was only fifty dollars. Mr. Roobush told us he wanted somebody to have it who knew Mrs. Roobush and himself and who would appreciate the old roadster. He told Fred and me how to use the choke and how to change the setting according to the temperature.

I think Mr. Roobush was almost as proud of the Model–A as he was of the little brick home he'd built so long ago.

He continued to live alone in that house after Mrs. Roobush died. He was an independent man who didn't want to burden anyone in his old age. His eyesight was failing and his hearing was all but gone. He was afraid to drive anymore. That's why he sold the car.

"That old car served us well, me and Mrs. Roobush. I hope you enjoy owning it, too. And I think it has a lot more life left in it than I have in these old bones," he told us.

Fifty dollars was almost a give-away price for the car. Mom could pay for it with one week's paycheck. I was grateful to Mr. Roobush. It was kind of him to sell it to us for so little. But after a day or two, my mind went on to other things and I stopped feeling grateful. In a couple of weeks, I thought about the car that was almost a gift and wondered what had happened to my gratitude.

Gratitude, I decided, must be the shortest-lived of all human emotions.

I had planned to drive to Mr. Roobush's house and show him my driver's license, once I got it. But he died before that was possible.

The car became mine and Fred's. By this time, hardly any Model–A Fords were still on the road. Most of our friends had never ridden in a rumble seat and they thoroughly enjoyed doing so.

Automobile advertising was right on target as far as we were concerned. This car had made us more popular with our friends.

Fred used the car on dates, but I didn't get the chance. Our garage caught fire and the Model–A Ford was destroyed. Firemen blamed the fire on neighborhood children playing with matches.

When I was in high school, a ghost of a memory came back to me, and I realized the person involved had been my father. What I remembered happened following the divorce when we still lived on State Street. Aunt Lolly had come to live with us. She had taken over my bed and I ended up on the davenport.

Whenever I had a bad dream, I would jump in bed with Mom. This was such a time. I woke up and knew someone was in the room with us. I got as close to Mom as I could, but the person slowly got closer and closer until I could make out a form standing over us.

I was afraid. So I remained still. After a while, because no harm had come to me, I must have stopped worrying and gone to sleep.

But in remembrance, I was convinced this had been my father. He had come one last time to see Mom. He must have stayed a long time watching us sleep. Then he went away for good.

Once, Fred said our father had a brother who lived in Cleveland and that Dad might be living with him. Fred talked about the two of us taking a bus to Cleveland in an attempt to find our father. But we were afraid it might upset Mom. So we never did it.

But I thought about my father a lot. Jam had lived with my parents almost from the time they were married. Dad later had to accept Jam's aged sister, as well. I thought about him and Mom having six children and having two of them die.

I thought about the Depression, that deep economic pit into which so many people languished, including Dad.

Someone asked me once if I ever forgave him for abandoning his family. But it had not occurred to me he had abandoned us, so I didn't think he was in need of my forgiveness.

Life heaped troubles on my father—buried him, really. Would I have handled it better, even as well?

One day, Mom and I were talking about my father.

"Your father was adopted," Mom told me for the first time.

"He never wanted to talk about it. And so we didn't. But he was adopted by Grandma and Grandpa Schroeder when he was a baby." My father's parents died before I was born, so I knew them only by name.

"What was his real name if it wasn't Schroeder?" I asked.

"It was Foster. But of course it became Schroeder when he was adopted as a baby."

"Why didn't you ever tell me this before?" I asked.

"Your dad was ashamed of it. I think he assumed he was really born out of wedlock, and he didn't want people to know."

I gradually got out of touch with my State Street friends during high school. Once in a while, I'd see one of them during class changes. Dick graduated a couple of years ahead of me. I never saw him or Ben again.

Maybe we no longer had any need to be friends. I don't know. I only know that for a long time, they were as important to me as family.

I think young people hear the distant pealing of wedding bells long before meeting the person of their dreams. And in preparation for life's responsibilities they move toward that compelling sound.

Blessings abound

With all of my summer and after-school work, I saved up a little more than one thousand dollars for college. I had sold shoes, bagged groceries, stocked grocery shelves, worked as a playground supervisor at a public park and taught tennis. The money I'd saved gave me a good start at Indiana University, where I worked as a bellhop at the Student Union hotel and cleared tables and washed dishes at the Kappa Delta Rho fraternity house. I also worked during the summers while in college. I sold high–end pots and pans, drew assembly drawings at a jet engine factory and made piston rings at another factory.

The summer before my senior year, I went to Fort Riley, Kansas, for advanced Army ROTC training camp.

I fell in love with a young woman, Helen Jane Probst, who was in several of my journalism classes. She grew up near Aurora, Indiana, which is on the Ohio River near Cincinnati. Her parents operated the Probst Milk Co. Helen's father, Eddie Probst, processed, bottled, and even delivered the milk to homes, schools and farms around Aurora. The summer after graduation, Helen and I were married at St. John Lutheran Church in Aurora.

Fred graduated as an architect from the University of Cincinnati. I figured that building and rebuilding all those model airplanes must have done something good for his brain. Mom was tremendously proud of Fred. But I think she was always confident he would apply himself in positive ways.

I don't think she was very sure about me. When I managed to get my name listed among those who would graduate, Mom was proud of me too.

Fred and I were the first ones in our family to get through college. We deserve possibly 10 percent of the credit. The other 90 percent goes to Mom.

She worked hard to give us the motivation to achieve. And somehow she fashioned for us an environment for success, though we were mostly surrounded by failure.

My sister, Mary Frances, stopped going to college in order to get married. After her children were grown, she returned to finish her teaching degree.

Mom and Newton Burger, my stepfather, attended my I.U. graduation ceremony at Bloomington. (They were married the summer before my college sophomore year.) Mom couldn't take enough snapshots with the pull-out accordion camera her parents had given her as a high school graduation gift. My grades never were nearly as good as Mom's, nor Fred's for that matter.

Parents do well if they manage to point children in the right direction. Mom had to work overtime with me and she had to do it pretty much by herself, though Jam helped as well as she could. Friends at church helped me, and my stepfather, brother, sisters and brothers–in–law helped as well as Mr. Briggs, my Scoutmaster. Dick Leary sure helped too, though he never knew it. We're pretty oblivious to how God keeps working through people, young and old, to share His love and grace.

My first job out of college was writing headlines for The *South Bend Tribune*. After an Army stint, I wrote for *The Dayton Journal Herald* and The *Columbus Citizen-Journal*.

Later, when I landed a job writing for the Bell System in Indianapolis, Helen and I attended Trinity Lutheran, the church which sponsored my old Scout troop. Three of our children started school at Trinity, which had been relocated to a large tract, way out on the East Side of Indianapolis. The area where the new church and school were built had been cornfields when I was growing up.

Most of my old friends had moved on. But Mr. Briggs, our Scoutmaster, was still a member.

Jam was ninety when she died. Nine years later, Mom suffered a stroke which paralyzed her right side. She died in a little over a year. She was seventy–one. Later, we heard my father had died at age seventy–nine. We also learned that through nearly a lifetime of effort, he had stopped drinking.

My sisters and brother and I talked about him. I supposed that in the days when Dad was a child, he would have been told little, if anything, about his biological parents. And most likely he would not know their true names. I asked the three of them whether they thought Dad's real name might actually have been Foster. Maybe it just meant that he was a foster child.

They were surprised—disbelieving is more like it— when confronted with the idea that Dad was adopted. Apparently, Mom had told only me about it.

But that was understandable. Dad had been around when my sisters were growing up. I believe he assumed he was born out of wedlock and he considered the subject taboo.

In some ways humankind improves over time and in some ways regresses. Examples of the latter are familiar enough. One way we seem to have vastly improved is in our view of children born out of wedlock. Whatever the circumstances surrounding Dad's birth and adoption, he had no reason for shame. Surely today, adopted children and their families are well beyond concern about this subject.

A new dawn

One warm Memorial Day, Mom, Jam, Fred and I caught the New Castle bus. This time we didn't get off in Greenfield but remained on all the way to New Castle.

Fred and I were born in this pretty town, as were my dead brother and sister. Both Mary Frances and Dorothy had grown up in New Castle.

I was just a month old when the family moved to Indianapolis. And I had never seen this pretty town where other family members had lived so much of their lives and experienced so much heartache.

We took a taxi to a greenhouse outside a cemetery, where Mom bought an urn, potting soil and some perennials. Then she got help from a caretaker and found the side-by-side graves of David and Joan.

Each had the same tiny lifespan. Joan died in 1926 when she was twenty–two months and one day old. David died nine years later, when he was twenty–two months and three days old. One year later I was born.

There were no headstones for them, only numbered concrete grave markers nearly grown over with grass.

"I always wanted to buy stones for the graves, but we couldn't afford it," Mom said as if in apology. She was able to buy headstones for them some years later.

I tried to think of Mom and Dad losing two children in death, but I knew I couldn't imagine the depths of such sorrow. I had seen photographs of Joan and David. They looked like beautiful, healthy children.

I felt sorry they had died, sorry because they had almost no life at all, sorry because I didn't have them around as a sister and brother, and very sorry because I knew their dying was such a terrible thing for Mom.

It's hard to love those you have not known. With Joan and David, I came closest in the realization that we shared parents. And I know how very much they were loved.

Mom planted the brightly colored flowers in the urn. And they looked pretty to me. She placed the urn between the two graves.

The sun flashed through the trees, like the twinkling of an eye, as we walked back to the entrance. A white marble angel stood guard nearby, the westerly sun back–lighting its countenance. But the face tilted upward over the graves, looking beyond a line separating earth and sky, as to a new dawn.

Time, like an ever-rolling stream,
Bears all its sons away;
They fly, forgotten as a dream
Dies, at the opening day.

O God, our help in ages past,
Our hope for years to come,
Be Thou our guide while life shall last,
And our eternal home.

—Isaac Watts, 1719

listen|imagine|view|experience

AUDIO BOOK DOWNLOAD INCLUDED WITH THIS BOOK!

In your hands you hold a complete digital entertainment package. Besides purchasing the paper version of this book, this book includes a free download of the audio version of this book. Simply use the code listed below when visiting our website. Once downloaded to your computer, you can listen to the book through your computer's speakers, burn it to an audio CD or save the file to your portable music device (such as Apple's popular iPod) and listen on the go!

How to get your free audio book digital download:

1. Visit www.tatepublishing.com and click on the e|LIVE logo on the home page.
2. Enter the following coupon code:
   2502-f9bd-4598-92fc-f0cd-cea2-0d3f-0c82
3. Download the audio book from your e|LIVE digital locker and begin enjoying your new digital entertainment package today!